Race, Racism and American Law

1984 Supplement

EDITORIAL ADVISORY BOARD

Little, Brown and Company
Law Book Division

Race, Racism and American Law

Second Edition

1984 Supplement

Derrick A. Bell, Jr.
Dean, University of Oregon
School of Law

Little, Brown and Company
Boston Toronto

Library of Congress Catalog Card No. 79-90940
ISBN 0-316-08815-3

JCI

Published simultaneously in Canada
by Little, Brown & Company (Canada) Limited

Printed in the United States of America

Contents

Table of Cases

Cases receiving more than cursory mention are in italic type.
Numbers are to pages.

Preface

The Second Edition of this text, published in 1980, was designed to provide more attention to large issues and trends, current as well as historical, in American racial and legal policy. Less emphasis was given to individual case opinions which were summarized, rather than printed in either full or edited form. That approach furthered pedagogical aims of the text and also lessened the need of frequent supplementation in a field where new decisions, while not pouring forth with the frequency of a decade ago, continue to appear at rates greater than those of many other areas of the law.

Even so, a supplement after four years cannot be faulted as premature. The lengthy period without updating is due less to any principle-based self-restraint than to my heavy administrative burdens at the University of Oregon Law School.

In fact, the publication of this Supplement is a testament to the perseverance of the editors at Little, Brown, and the dedicated work of two student research and writing assistants, Ms. Allison Blakeley, Oregon, J.D. 1982, and Ms. Suzanne Anderson, now a third-year law student at Oregon. A small bow is also in order to the microcomputer, a new technology that brings to the life of the harried legal text writer much assistance, as well as some aggravation.

Derrick Bell

July 1984

Part I
Racial Patterns in American Law

Chapter 1
American Racism and the Uses of History

§1.1.1 *Introduction to the Supplement*

At least one goal of Race, Racism and American Law, Second Edition (hereinafter Second Edition), was to establish an approach or method of interpreting existing cases as well as the book's approach toward consideration of those cases, so that post-publication developments in the field would simply provide more up-to-date variations on already well-established themes.

The number of new cases and other civil rights activities have not maintained the headlong pace of the 1960's and early 1970's. Unhappily for civil rights advocates, much of what has occurred in the period since the Second Edition was published in mid-1980, has served to give substance to the generally pessimistic tone that some reviewers of Race, Racism and American Law, found to prevail in the book. Fatalism in the area of American race relations comes easily and without invitation to any serious discussion of the subject. And when history is blended with contemporary events, rosy optimism about either the present or the future is simply difficult to justify.

Quite appropriately, history is the perspective from which two thoughtful reviews of the Second Edition have been written.[1] The comments and criticisms they contain provide a worthwhile supplement to the introductory positions set out in Chapter 1. The views expressed by the reviewers, particularly those that question positions taken in the Second Edition, should add new dimensions to class discussion and student understanding of a subject that grows more, rather than less, complex with the passing years.

1. Freeman, Book Review, *Race and Class: The Dilemma of Liberal Reform*, 90 Yale L.J. 1880 (1980); Willhelm, Book Review, *The Supreme Court: A Citadel for White Supremacy*, 79 Mich. L. Rev. 847 (1981).

§1.12.1 Freeman, Race and Class: The Dilemma of Liberal Reform

Professor Alan Freeman's insightful explanation of the differing perspectives on civil rights held by blacks and whites added much to Chapter 9 of the Second Edition.[2] He acknowledges in his review that court decisions in the last several years have been far less helpful than the earlier precedent-making cases that set legal standards enabling measurable gains, even though, in retrospect, many of the early cases promised more than they produced.[3] Freeman finds that despite the presence of doctrinal materials in the Second Edition, "the book in its dominant tone is impatient with legal doctrine and despairing," offering half-heartedly, legal arguments unlikely ever to be adopted by the courts. He predicts that some readers will find the book's emphasis cynical while others will see it as realistic. But he wonders, "what is one supposed to do in teaching this course?"[4]

He explains his dilemma. Students enrolling in a civil rights course are usually those most committed to seeking social justice through law. "Yet," he says, "if the truth seems so hopeless and dismal, and the generation of more legal argument so pointless, then one is dealing with something other than the usual law school enterprise of helping students to fashion a measure of craft, skill, and insight to deal with needs and hopes of social life."[5]

There is, Freeman feels, a need to pierce the veil of presuppositions on which civil rights doctrine relies. That is,

> — a world of autonomous and responsive law; shared values such as individualism and color-blindness; monolithic whiteness or blackness rather than class structured societal divisions; and gradual linear civil rights progress is assumed.

Freeman would close the gap between "the mythical world of legal doctrine and the real world in history":

> — a world where law is more responsive to power than to powerlessness; where values are contradictory, conflicting, and bound up with patterns of domination and hierarchy; where class relationships exist alongside racial ones; and where cyclical failure is as plausible as linear progress.

2. §9.13.1 summarizing the blacks' "victim" perspective and the "perpetrator" views of whites. See, Freeman, *Legitimizing Racial Discrimination Through Antidiscrimination Law: A Critical Review of Supreme Court Doctrine*, 62 Minn. L. Rev. 209, 1052-1053 (1978).

3. Freeman, *supra*, at 1881-1884.

4. *Id.* at 1886.

5. *Id.*

Freeman sees a number of possible strategies:

Strategy One — "Playing the Game." Self-consciously manipulate legal doctrine to achieve whatever can be gained that will improve the lives of some, but without any real hope that structural change can come through litigation and legislation under the existing political structure.

Strategy Two — Politicizing the Game. Extending Strategy One to maximize the politicization of the doctrinal activity, i.e., "pushing the legal forms for explicitly political reasons to reveal contradictions and limits, promote public awareness, and even win cases."

But Freeman finds even these strategies preserve what he calls the "myths of liberal reform." Neither obviates the need to immerse civil rights doctrine in social and historical reality. He then admits that "it is one thing to call for — and show the need for — the historicization of civil rights law, and quite another to write the history." In the balance of his review, Professor Freeman attempts to provide a concrete historical account to replace what is exposed as inadequate.[6]

The Second Edition, Freeman finds, fails to provide a coherent account that would place civil rights law in its historical and social setting. He notes that at many points, the question of race is permitted to intersect with that of class. He cites as examples textual questions as to whether "the capitalistic class structure [could] maintain itself without the scapegoat role which blacks have filled for 300 years."[7] Freeman also refers to several variants of my oft-expressed maxim that "blacks will never get free until poor whites get smart." By this statement, I refer to the fact that ruling class whites, not blacks, maintain most whites in a subordinate status.[8]

Admittedly, my references to the intersections of race and class were not intended to be definitive, but rather were offered as a motive for broadening the discussion of race that too frequently focuses on black victims of racism, and assumes that the harm they have suffered was the result of the total insensitivity, if not downright perfidy, of whites. But, from the Founding Fathers' decision to sanction slavery in the Constitution to the present day, economics has been a strong factor — perhaps the crucial factor — in policymaking involving race.

Freeman, though, would supplement and strengthen my tentative suggestions of a race/class connection in American racial issues. He finds some

6. *Id.* at 1887-1888.

7. *Id.* at 1888. Freeman counts 27 references of this type. See Second Edition, at pp. 7, 51, 64, 66, 85-86, 93, 267, 399, 435, 437, 438, 439, 443, 454-456, 457, 492, 530, 536, 553-556, 589, 589-591, 611-612, 632-633, 636, 656-665.

8. For example, the concern at p. 492 of the Second Edition, that referenda on civil rights issues are damaging to blacks because "lower-class whites will often support referenda advancing middle-class values, even to the detriment of their own economic interests," thereby isolating blacks from "potential class allies."

help in Professor George Fredrickson's recently published comparative history of race relations in the United States and South Africa from the seventeenth to the twentieth century.[9] The history of racial policies in both countries, Professor Fredrickson found, was affected in a major way by the tensions or divisions within the white social structure. "The degradation of non-whites frequently served to bind together the white population, or some segment of it, to create a sense of community of solidarity that could become a way of life and not simply a cover for economic exploitation."[10]

With regard to the American South, Fredrickson reaches conclusions quite like those of historians quoted in Chapter One of the Second Edition. He finds that the fact that most whites were not slaveholders was a critical factor in explaining the rigidity of racial distinctions because "racial privilege could and did serve as a compensation for class disadvantage."[11] He also observes that the failure of the First Reconstruction could have been the product of the conflict between the Radical Republicans' middle-class idealism and their concern about the prospect of class conflict brought out by the emergent labor movement. The conflict, he suggests, revealed the ideological limitations of their egalitarianism. Freeman then quotes Fredrickson's perspective of the relationship between industrialism and racial discrimination, which he suggests (and I agree) is applicable to modern racial policymaking:

> My assumption is that economic discrimination along racial lines would not have developed and persisted in the industrial era to the extent that it did if it had not served in some way the material interests of industrial capitalists and skilled white workers. But it is difficult to account for the specific nature of racial caste or exclusion in industry without reference to pre-existing beliefs about the character, capacity, and social status of nonwhites. Furthermore, political and legal developments of a partially autonomous nature could impinge on the economic order in such a way as to influence significantly, for better or worse, the life chances of blacks or other nonwhites in the industrial arena.[12]

Freeman finds Fredrickson's explanation far more convincing than the conventional Marxist analyses of racism that "make the mistake of *either* collapsing racism into a problem of class domination generally, as if it were nothing more than an incidental consequence of evolving capitalism (thereby denying its experiential reality), *or* treating racism as a mode of oppression so autonomous from capitalist social and economic relationships

9. G. Fredrickson, White Supremacy (1981).
10. *Id.* at 70.
11. *Id.* at 87.
12. *Id.* at 205.

that it can be rectified by aiming at a target of oppressors that appears as (classless?) 'white society.' "[13]

Contrary to traditional Marxist theories, Freeman believes that "the goal of civil rights law is to offer a credible measure of tangible progress without in any way disturbing class structure generally."[14] Thus, the interests of ruling classes will be advanced by "bourgeoisifying" a sufficient number of minority people in order to transform those people into active and visible legitimators of the underlying and basically unchanged social structure. Freeman would agree with William J. Wilson[15] and Thomas Sowell[16] that some anti-discrimination strategies like affirmative action contribute to this result by "improving the lot of a small number of middle-class minorities while consigning vast numbers of lower class minority people, to perhaps permanent underclass status."

The question for Freeman is not whether racism is different from class divisions generally — he concedes that it is — but whether "anything significant can be done about the admittedly unique problems of racism without paying attention to class structure and the forces that maintain it." He believes that a measurable portion of American society has committed itself to remedying the historical problem of race, but has not made even the pretense of such a commitment with respect to class.

Freeman's quote is significant. It offers an explanation why so many sincerely advanced measures intended to reduce discrimination are diluted in their implementation, and why even though large portions of the white population benefit directly or indirectly from the removal of barriers harmful to blacks, such as too rigid college admissions standards, they remain at least ambivalent about such reforms and, as with affirmative action in the

13. Freeman, *supra* note 1 at 1891. He identifies the "reserve army of labor" view under which racism serves to hold down wages generally by offering capitalists a ready market of cheap unskilled labor. He sees some truth in this explanation, but questions whether the "reserve army" theory either serves, or is even consistent with, contemporary capitalism where an unskilled work force is a liability and even a threat to the modern corporate state.

Similarly, the notion that racism serves to divide the working class, to create internal conflicts and antagonisms that frustrate the creation of genuine class consciousness essential to racial reform, also seems incomplete to Freeman. Again, though he agrees racism may have served this function, it neither explains the historical development of racism as a unique form of oppression, nor reveals why racism is needed given the presence of widespread belief systems like the "liberal" tradition, media-induced consumerism, and equality of opportunity, and occasional bouts of hysterical nationalism. *Id.* at 1892.

14. *Id.* at 1894. This view accords with those asserted by Robert Allen, who finds a similarity in the post-*Brown* elevation of some blacks in this country to the policy of creating class divisions among the subjugated people utilized by the European colonizers in Africa. See, §9.13.3 of the Second Edition, quoting from R. Allen, Black Awakening in Capitalist America (1969).

15. W. Wilson, The Declining Significance of Race (1978).

16. T. Sowell, Black Education: Myths and Tragedies (1982).

work place, tend to be quite hostile to them. In the application of some reforms, Freeman views opposition by whites as understandable as well as predictable.

Thus, for Freeman, there is no question but that the disappointed white worker who loses out to a minority under an affirmative action policy *is* a class victim. Inevitably, he warns, the effort to remedy racism in a class society with a stagnant or dwindling economy means that burdens of displacement will fall heavily on powerless whites. For this reason, he agrees with history-based conclusions reached in the Second Edition and by Professor Fredrickson that the assault on racism under such circumstances will come to a halt, lest it unleash too much rage or expose the reality of class relationships.

He concludes, with hardly more optimism than he found in the Second Edition, "There is nothing particularly radical about the goal of ending racial discrimination. The goal would be achieved if nonwhites were stratified across American society in percentages similar to whites. The class structure would remain intact." He wonders (as I do), though, "whether even that modest, liberal reformist goal is at all achievable without a radical confrontation with the truth of American history and society, past and present."[17] For us both, the question of "whether" is of no more interest than those of "when" and "how."

§1.12.2 Willhelm, *The Supreme Court: A Citadel for White Supremacy*

Despite the premature victory celebrations by liberals in the mid-1960s, the racism-free, egalitarian society has not arrived, and Professor Willhelm asserts that the growing disparity in the statistical indicia of economic status between whites and blacks provides bottom-line proof that the advent of racial equality remains a future event. The question is: Why has not the generally accepted doctrine of equal opportunity served to liberate blacks?[18]

In response, Willhelm first rejects as unsatisfactory and unsupported the self-interest motivations suggested in the Second Edition.[19] He doubts that there were Cold War fears that segregation at home would hinder the country's efforts to win the allegiance of nonwhite peoples emerging from colonial rule. World opinion had little impact on the government's conduct in the war in Vietnam. Nor, in his view, can we explain the equality doctrine by any proof that whites were responding to blacks' heightened expectations based on blacks' participation in World War II to make the world

17. *Id.* at 1895.
18. Willhelm, Book Review, 79 Mich. L. Rev. 847 (1981).
19. *See* §7.11.3 White Self-Interest as a Support for *Brown*.

safe for democracy. America entered World War I with similar slogans, and yet there was a resurgence of racism after the conflict. Willhelm claims a heightened demand for labor, and not an ideological commitment to democracy, prompted wartime concessions to blacks. And, he adds, as far as segregation inhibiting the industrialization of the South, materials in the Second Edition document that racial segregation prevailed in the North throughout industrialization.

Why did the country adopt the ideology of equality if not as a concession to blacks? Willhelm says that "changes in the economy made the ideology of Equality an appropriate tool to preserve White privilege, just as earlier changes had led to the demise of slavery and the rise of segregation."[20] He does not see this transformation as conscious any more than was the transformation from slavery to segregation. Rather, it occurred gradually over time. Even so, he cites the continued segregation of most schools and housing, and the racial disparities in income as indications that make it apparent that "constitutional Equality is merely another form of White domination."

Like Professor Freeman, Willhelm believes that while slavery and segregation rested on the need to exploit black labor, whites now produce wealth through the exploitation of technology, and not needing blacks, feel free to offer them "equal opportunity." In support of his charge that blacks are increasingly being disgorged from the labor force as surplusage in the modern, computerized economy, Willhelm cites figures that the percentage of black males out of the labor market altogether — those neither working nor seeking work — doubled, from 20 percent in the mid-sixties to the present 40 percent.[21]

The Second Edition, according to Willhelm, does not go far enough in pointing out that constitutional decisions have not produced socioeconomic improvements for blacks and have not eradicated racism that remains "embedded in the fabric of American Society, . . ." The Constitution itself is a racist document, and the very idea of equal treatment for blacks and whites is racist because it fails to take account of over three hundred years of racist oppression. Blacks remain under the domination of whites. Only the doctrines that sanction that domination have changed.

20. Willhelm, *supra* note 18, at 850.

21. *Id.* at 851. The failure of blacks to gain education for skilled, technological jobs does not explain the figures, Willhelm maintains. Unemployment for blacks relative to whites increases with level of education. "Among persons aged sixteen through twenty-four in 1979, 16.4 percent of White high school dropouts were unemployed while the figure for Blacks stood at 31.6 percent for a Black-White ratio of 1.9; 8.5 percent of White high school graduates were unemployed in contrast to 21.3 percent of Blacks, for a ratio of 2.5; and unemployment among White college graduates amounted to 4 percent while black college graduates had an unemployment rate of 17.1, for a ratio of 4.3." *Id.*

Willhelm explains that in the plantation economy, the Protestant ethic that legitimated the worldly accumulation of wealth also sanctioned slavery. In the industrial era, social Darwinism sanctioned the right of the rich to their wealth and also justified the segregation of blacks. Today, neither religion nor social Darwinism is sufficient to justify the continued degradation of blacks. This status must be sanctioned on the constitutional ground of equality. This myth of equality within a context of oppression simply provides a veneer for more oppression. This oppression in the labor market and the growing socioeconomic gap causes Willhelm to have fears about the continued existence of black life in America. With no powerful whites willing to protect blacks because of their value as labor, predictable future ghetto uprisings could provide the excuse for some police and other officials for the elimination of blacks who resist military rule over the ghetto. Military retaliation, Willhelm warns, will not recognize class distinctions. All blacks, regardless of class, will be the enemy.

Thus Professor Willhelm shares, on the basis of different data, the pessimism permeating Professor Freeman's analysis of racism in America. One wonders whether the picture for the future will be brightened by a massive utilization of the vote by blacks as has occurred in Chicago, Philadelphia, and several other cities where blacks have been elected as mayors, and have become a major force in local politics.

The decisions reported in this Supplement, most of which were decided after these two reviews were prepared for publication, do little to reveal that the gloomy assessments of Professors Freeman and Willhelm are excessive. There is a continued willingness on the part of courts to grant rather narrow relief on the presentation of clear proof of discrimination. And while racial bias in a myriad of more or less subtle forms continues to flourish, the barriers of class and past discrimination, rendered invisible by the seemingly liberating but actually stifling policy of equality, have become insurmountable for literally millions of blacks.

These, then, are the problems. Out of those problems must come solutions. There have been no easy avenues to salvation for America's ongoing racial dilemma, and even the hard ways have not guaranteed progress or the meaningful hope of progress. The reviewers note the pessimistic tone of the Second Edition, but, in effect, are critical that it does not cover other areas of racial policy that would render it more pessimistic than it is.

It is not, however, the goal of the text to provide a social formula that would solve the racial issues that beset the country. Rather it is to review those issues in all their political and economic dimensions, and from that vantage point utilize lawyering skills to determine where we might go from there. The goal for us, as it was for all those since the era of slavery who labored and sacrificed for freedom, was not to guarantee an end to racism, but to work forcefully toward that end.

Chapter 2 Interracial Sex and Marriage

§2.1.1 Updating the Mixed Marriage Data and Controversy

Interracial dating remains common on at least the more progressive college and high school campuses and, according to U.S. Census reports, there is a growing number of interracial married couples in this country. Between 1960 and 1970, the number of interracial marriages jumped by 108 percent (from 148,000 to 310,000). They increased another 36 percent (310,000 to 421,000) from 1970 to 1977, and from 1977 to 1981, climbed from 421,000 to 639,000. Black/white couples constituted 132,000 of the interracial couples in 1981.[1]

The steadily increasing figures do not much alter the fact that the 639,000 interracial couples in 1981 represent only 1.28 percent of all 49.8 million married couples. But while the percentage of interracial marriages is a minuscule percentage of all marriages, the acceptance level, if not the legality, of interracial sex and marriage remains a quite controversial area of American life for both whites and nonwhites.

There are relatively few new cases in this field. The main areas of litigation involve employees or househunters who assert that they have been discriminated against because they are married to or are on intimate terms with a person of another race. There have also been a few interracial adoption cases.

1. 1970 and 1977 figures from U.S. Bureau of the Census, Current Population Reports, Series P-23, No. 77, *Perspectives on American Husbands and Wives,* U.S. Government Printing Office, Washington, D.C. 1978 (p. 7-10).

1981 figures from U.S. Bureau of the Census, Current Population Reports, Series P-20, No. 371, *Household and Family Characteristics: March 1981,* U.S. Government Printing Office, Washington, D.C. 1982 (p. 163-164).

Of the 421,000 interracial couples in 1977, 125,000 were black/white couples. Couples in this category increased by 60,000 or 92 percent over the 1970 figure. Three-fourths of the black/white couples in 1977 had a black husband and a white wife. And by 1981, the percentage of black husband, white wife couples had increased to almost 80 percent. *Id.*

Of course, the litigation receiving most recent media attention is the challenges to church-school policies barring black students or limiting the social relations of black and white students. These policies are justified by those who espouse them as being based on religious belief and thus protected by the First Amendment's "free exercise" clause. In the Second Edition, cases involving opposition to interracial association were frequently discussed in the subject areas where the cases arose (housing in Chapter 8, or public accommodations in Chapter 3) but upon reflection, discrimination on the basis of interracial status is sufficiently unique to warrant coverage in Chapter 2.

§2.6.1 Interracial Couples and Housing Discrimination

Ku Klux Klan members expressed their opposition to interracial relationships by firing into a residence that was the home of two black men and two white women. These actions, together with other harassment of NAACP officials, led to the conviction of the KKK members for intimidating and interfering with persons exercising federally protected rights in violation of the Fair Housing Act of 1968.[2] It is easy to dismiss such totally irresponsible actions as "typical of the Klan," but under those robes there are men, human beings with emotions and fears like the rest of us. When human beings, motivated solely by the information that a black man or woman is cohabiting with a white woman or man at a certain address, arm themselves, sally forth and shoot blindly into that residence, what precisely are they trying to kill? What message are they trying to convey?

Fortunately, few Americans feel as strongly about interracial cohabitation as did the Klan members in the *United States v. Johns* case, but the facts in *Oliver v. Shelly*[3] are all too typical. It was not remarkable that the court there found a violation of both Section 1982 and the Fair Housing Act when the landlord admitted that one factor in his refusal of an apartment to an interracial couple was "concern of tension caused by their presence."[4] Surely, the court was right, but just as surely, the landlord's concerns were likely not without basis even 15 years after enactment of the Fair Housing Act. Indeed, the presence of an interracial couple, especially if the man is black, will give rise to more "tension" than if both spouses were black.

One wonders why this should be so. Whatever the accuracy of the psychological theory that black males see in their seduction of white women

2. United States v. Johns, 615 F.2d 672 (5th Cir. 1980). The court relied on §3631 of the Act.

3. 538 F. Supp. 600 (S.D. Tex. 1982).

4. *Id.* at 602. Even assuming the influence of other factors on the landlord's refusal, the court said such factors did not diminish the seriousness of the violation. "We find no acceptable place in the law for partial racial discrimination." *Id.*

as a form of rebellion against white society's strange miscegenation mystique (See Second Edition §2.3), a black man who chooses a white wife would seem to have made the ultimate commitment to an integrated existence. Can it be that his willingness to make this commitment evidences a societal boldness that is in itself threatening?

On the other hand, the "tensions" so feared by the landlord may simply be the normal reaction to what for many tenants will be the new, the unusual, and, for some, the bizarre. For those whites who don't move, the interracial couple will likely be little cause for special concern after a few months. Unhappy white tenants might respond that they could probably adjust to a halfway house in their residential neighborhood too, but they are living where they are precisely to avoid the necessity for such adjustments.

§2.7.1 *Interracial Adoptions and the American Indian Child Welfare Act of 1978*

The problems minority groups face as they seek to maintain their cultural uniqueness within a dominant, different, and often hostile society are universal. Section 2.7 of the Second Edition referred to writings by black social workers who condemned interracial adoptions as "a growing threat to the preservation of the black family." They urge that standards for adoption be eased so that black families, willing to adopt, would not be excluded because they are unable to meet traditional qualifications on age, health, income, marital status, home size, and other criteria that exclude those who are not substantial members of the middle class.

Native American groups have experienced similar problems in preserving their cultural heritage. According to one commentator, Manuel P. Guerrero,[5] the policy of destroying Indian culture and tribal integrity by removing Indian children from their families and tribal settings was set even before the country became a nation. By the end of the nineteenth century, sending Indian children away to distant boarding schools to "civilize" and educate them had become customary among the tribes. Often the removal of children was coerced by agents of the Department of Indian Affairs.

Currently, the removal of Indian children to boarding schools continues, but even larger numbers of children are removed from their homes for purposes of foster care and adoption. Studies in 1969 and 1974 of states with large Indian populations indicate that 25-35 percent of all Indian children are separated from their families and placed in foster homes or institutions.

5. Guerrero, *Indian Child Welfare Act of 1978*, 7 Am. Ind. L. Rev. 51 (1979).

According to one writer, "American Indian families face vastly greater risks of involuntary separation than are typical of society as a whole."[6] Mr. Guerrero concurs, stating that the wholesale separation of Indian children from their families ranks among the most tragic and destructive aspects of contemporary Indian life. He reports:

> State intrusion in parent-child relationships within the Indian culture impedes the ability of the tribe to perpetuate itself and is ultimately an unjustified coerced assimilation into the larger society. . . . (T)he Indian way of life is a unique expression of an identifiable but highly complex culture apart from the non-Indian world. It is a culture which has at its core a persistent talent for preservation and survival. Among other aspects, it is inculcated with the concept known as the extended family, which is largely misunderstood by white America.[7]

Black social workers opposed to interracial adoption of black children would likely adopt Mr. Guerrero's statement in whole. It is as applicable to black as to Indian families. They would certainly recognize his reports that social workers, untrained in Indian cultural values and social norms, make decisions inappropriate to Indian family patterns, judge the fitness of an Indian family by white middle-class values, and thus discover neglect and abandonment where none exists.

In late 1978, Congress, responding to recommendations of the American Indian Review Commission, enacted the Indian Child Welfare Act.[8] The Act is premised on the fact that Indian tribes, as sovereign governments, have a vital interest in any decision as to whether Indian children should be separated from their families. With a few exceptions, the Act gives the Indian tribe, and more specifically the Indian tribal court, exclusive jurisdiction over child custody proceedings where the Indian child is residing or domiciled on the reservation.

State courts having jurisdiction over an Indian child custody proceeding are directed by the Act to transfer such proceeding to an appropriate tribal court. Either parent may veto such transfer so as to enable the state court to insure that the rights of the child, the parents, and the tribe are fully protected. Various procedural protections are provided, including adequate notice and right to counsel, to further the goals of the Act.

Parental rights may not be easily terminated, and a party seeking foster care placement or termination of parental rights over an Indian child must satisfy the court that positive efforts have been made to provide assistance designed to prevent the breakup of Indian families. Section 1915 of the Act addresses the adoptive placement of Indian children subsequent to the ter-

6. McCartney, *The American Indian Child-Welfare Crisis: Cultural Genocide or First Amendment Preservation*, 7 Col. Human Rights L. Rev. 529, 530 (1975).

7. *See* Guerrero *supra* note 5, at 53.

8. 25 U.S.C. §§1901-1963 (1982).

mination of parental rights, and provides that "a preference shall be given, in the absence of good cause to the contrary, to a placement with (1) a member of the child's extended family; (2) other members of the Indian child's tribe; or (3) other Indian families."[9]

Although the Act may help preserve the ethnic identity of Indian children who are placed out for adoption, its provisions are largely procedural and deal only with children who have been removed from their families. Professor Russel Barsh stresses the need for substantive support to Indian families and the tribes to prevent the break-up of existing families.[10]

§2.7.2 *Interracial Influences on Custody Cases*

During 1982, the case of *Blackburn v. Blackburn,*[11] became a minor *cause celebre.* Kathleen Blackburn came to Millen, Georgia to marry a local boy, had one son, Nicholas, divorced her husband, and began taking the infant child to her job and to late-night parties. She had an affair with a married, black police officer, the result of which was a second child. Her former husband's parents, outraged over her conduct, went to court and obtained an order awarding custody of Nicholas to them. The local judge, while insisting that race was not a factor in the verdict, told one of several reporters who descended on the town to cover the story, "this town just isn't ready for that sort of integration."[12]

Several outside organizations petitioned the Georgia Supreme Court on Kathleen's behalf. They argued that custody cannot be terminated because a child might have more advantages with other guardians. The grandparents claim Kathleen failed to "provide necessaries" and was rearing their grandchild under "immoral, obscene . . . influences likely to degrade his moral character." But the Georgia Supreme Court found the evidence fell short of demonstrating present unfitness such as to justify their termination of Kathleen's rights in her son. Without condoning her relationship resulting in the birth of an illegitimate child, and while recognizing that "society may stigmatize Nicholas because his sibling is illegitimate."

9. 25 U.S.C. §1915(a) (1982). Under §1915(a), the quoted provision is to be read as a preference for keeping the Indian child in the tribe rather than a preclusion of placement with a non-Indian family. Similar provisions are provided for foster care or preadoptive placements. For a detailed review of all the provisions of the Act, *see* Guerrero, *supra* note 5.

10. Barsh, *Indian Child Welfare Act of 1978: A Critical Analysis,* 31 Hastings L.J. 1287 (1980). Barsh takes a more pessimistic view of the Act than does the Guerrero piece. He agrees with the aims of the Act, but feels that it does not do enough, is poorly drafted, and will be ineffective even within its too limited scope.

11. 249 Ga. 689, 292 S.E.2d 821 (1982).

12. *Blackburn v. Blackburn, Newsweek,* May 17, 1982, at 105.

that fact was deemed insufficient evidence of unfitness to justify severance of a parent-child custodial relationship.

Avoiding the interracial overtones of the case, the court cited an earlier decision to the effect that a parent's natural rights in a child cannot be terminated because that child might have better financial, educational, or even moral advantages elsewhere. While lacking legal grounds, the grandparents' concern that Kathleen was an unfit mother would have gained moral force had they sought custody of Kathleen's second child as well as Nicholas. But perhaps this is more than one could expect of grandparents even if race was not a motive for their action.

More recently, a Florida court in a custody case with quite similar facts awarded a white father custody of his child after his former wife first lived with and later married a black man. The Supreme Court reversed in *Palmore v. Sidoti,*[13] holding unanimously that racial considerations cannot be a determinative factor in child custody decisions. Linda Sidoti Palmore, a white woman, was awarded custody of her daughter, Melanie, when she and Anthony Sidoti, also white, were divorced in 1980. When she later married Clarence Palmore, a black man, Mr. Sidoti applied for a change of custody.

The Circuit Court for Hillsborough County, Florida, ruled that though both parents had chosen "respectable" new spouses, and though society has made strides in "bettering relations between the races," it was inevitable that Melanie would "suffer from the social stigmatization that is sure to come" if she remained with her mother. The court also noted that Mrs. Palmore had cohabited with her present husband before their marriage. "Such action," the lower court found, "tended to place gratification of her own desires ahead of her concern for the child's future welfare."

The Florida Court of Appeals affirmed without opinion,[14] and Mrs. Palmore appealed to the United States Supreme Court, arguing that the custody decision violated equal protection by punishing her for marrying outside her race. The United States Solicitor General, the NAACP, the Women's Legal Defense Fund, and other organizations filed amicus briefs on behalf of Mrs. Palmore.

Writing for the Court, Chief Justice Burger acknowledged that state court custody decisions are unlikely candidates for Supreme Court review, but important federal concerns were raised by the lower court's finding regarding the damaging impact on the child of remaining in a racially mixed home. Taking the court's findings and rationale at face value, Burger found it clear that "outcome would have been different had petitioner married a Caucasian male of similar respectability."

The state, Burger said, has a duty of the highest order to protect the interests of minor children and has a substantial governmental interest for

13. 426 So. 2d 34 (Fla. Ct. App. 1982), *rev'd* 104 S. Ct. 1879 (1984).
14. 426 So. 2d 34 (Fla. Ct. App. 1982).

purposes of the Equal Protection Clause. And, a child living with a step-parent of another race may face a variety of stresses and pressures due to the fact that racial and ethnic prejudices do exist. But citing the early residential neighborhood segregation case of *Buchanan v. Warley*,[15] the Chief Justice wrote that the reality of private biases and the possible injury they might inflict are not permissible considerations for removal of an infant child from the custody of its natural mother.

"Whatever problems racially-mixed households may pose for children in 1984," Chief Justice Burger said, "can no more support a denial of constitutional rights than could the stresses that residential integration was thought to entail in 1917. The effects of racial prejudice, however real, cannot justify a racial classification removing an infant child from the custody of its natural mother found to be an appropriate person to have such custody."[16]

§2.9 *Racism Hypo: Proposed Legislation: An American Black Child Welfare Act*

John and Mary Robinson are a black couple living modestly in a mainly black, middle-class suburb in Queens, New York. After 25 years with the Post Office, John took retirement at 55 with a disability due to chronic high blood pressure. His wife is 50 and in good health.

They have no children of their own, but became foster parents of twin boys and their older sister five years ago, after the parents of the three children were killed in a traffic accident. The children and their parents had lived next door to the Robinsons, and the children thought of the Robinsons as grandparents. The Robinsons had often taken care of the children when they were infants, and after the death of their parents tried unsuccessfully to adopt them. The state agency rejected their adoption efforts because of their age, the size of their income, John's health, and the lack of adequate bedroom space in their small house.

Under agency rules that favor adoption over foster placement, information about the three children (the twins are now 8 years old, and their

15. 245 U.S. 60 (1917). In *Buchanan*, the Court had said:

> It is urged that this proposed segregation will promote the public peace by preventing race conflicts. Desirable as this is, and important as is the preservation of the public peace, this aim cannot be accomplished by laws or ordinances which deny rights created or protected by the Federal Constitution. *Id.* at 1881.

16. *Id.* at 1882. Does the Court's language seal the fate of the proposed legislation suggested in the Racism Hypo "An American Black Welfare Act," set out below?

sister is 10) was sent to all adoption agencies across the country. A request to adopt all three children was received and subsequently approved from a family, the Meanwells, living in a small town in western Oregon. The adopting couple have two children of their own and have within the last few years adopted an Asian child and a black child. They meet all requirements of the state adoption agency. The children themselves wish to remain with the Robinsons and want to live in the area in which they have gone to school, made friendships, and feel at home.

The Robinsons, with the help of a legal aid lawyer, tried to challenge the adoptions in state court. They asserted that they would be good parents, and expressed concern about the children's future welfare if they were moved across country to an all-white area where, whatever the parental skills of the adopting family, the children would be removed from their culture and would be unable to learn the survival skills still required by blacks in a racist society. The state court dismissed the challenge on procedural grounds without reaching the substantive issues raised by the Robinsons.

Black social welfare groups have gathered dozens of case histories like that of the Robinsons and presented them to the state legislature as support for a bill they call the American Black Child Welfare Act. As with its Indian counterpart, the bill creates a preference, albeit in the state courts, for keeping black children in either black homes or homes where one parent is black. It provides for an easing of adoption standards that reflect middle-class values to the extent that such standards do not relate directly to the health, safety, and well-being of the adoptive child.

Civil libertarians, and some civil rights groups as well, are horrified by the measure, which they view as an unnecessary legislative recognition of racial patterns and practices they are committed to ending. They believe that all children should be adopted by the most qualified family and that the race of either the children or the adopting parents should be of little or no significance. They admit that racism is still a factor in the lives of blacks and other minorities, but that white as well as black families can adequately prepare minority children for dealing with this problem. They pledge that if the measure is enacted they will challenge it in the federal courts on constitutional grounds.

Law Firm A is asked to represent before the legislature the interests of the black social welfare groups supporting the American Black Child Welfare Act.

Law Firm B has been retained to represent the civil liberties groups who oppose the measure.[17]

17. This racism hypo is based roughly on a quite similar case reported in a Eugene, Oregon newspaper. See, "Contested Adoption Request Shifts to Lane County Court," *Eugene Register Guard*, Feb. 6, 1983, p.1.

§2.10 *Religious Belief and Interracial Social Contact*

For the last few years, the public has been debating the issue fought by churches and civil rights groups for more than a decade: to what extent churches operating private schools with racially discriminatory policies are exempt from the desegregation mandate of *Brown v. Board of Education.* And, as if the interspersion of statutory and First Amendment questions were not enough, the Reagan administration has determined to make the issue a blatantly political one.[18] Litigation on the question stretches back to the late 1960's, but public attention has been drawn to two challenges filed by fundamentalist church sects. Appealing to the Supreme Court from adverse rulings below, the basic issue presented the Court was whether the Internal Revenue Code can be read to require the denial or the revocation of tax-exempt status to private religious schools that engage in racial discrimination based on religious belief.

In the final weeks of its 1982 term, the Supreme Court responded with a firm "*No*" in *Bob Jones University v. United States.*[19] In an opinion by Chief Justice Burger in which only Justice Rehnquist dissented, the Court found the governmental interest in eradicating racial discrimination in education compelling, fundamental, overriding, and substantially outweighing whatever burden denial of tax benefits places on petitioners' exercise of

18. The Internal Revenue Service was under strong pressure to conform its regulations to decisions like Green v. Connally, 330 F. Supp. 1150 (D.D.C. 1971), *aff'd sub nom.* Coit v. Green, 404 U.S. 997 (1971), barring federal tax exempt status unless the schools demonstrated a publicized nondiscriminatory admissions policy. *See* 2nd Ed. §3.9, n.3. The Internal Revenue Service announced that it could "no longer legally justify allowing tax-exempt status to private schools which practice racial discrimination. . . ."

Then, in 1982, as it developed the government's position in the *Bob Jones* and *Goldsboro Christian School* cases pending before the Supreme Court, the Treasury Department, with the advice of the Justice Department, reversed its interpretation of the Internal Revenue Code. It announced that, in the absence of specific statutes authorizing such a policy, it would no longer revoke or deny tax-exempt status for religious, charitable, educational, or scientific organizations on the grounds of their nonconformity with fundamental policies — including the national policy against racial discrimination.

The change in policy evoked strong protests from civil rights groups, and when the government withdrew from the appeals in the *Bob Jones* and *Goldsboro Christian School* cases, the Supreme Court appointed former Department of Transportation secretary, William Coleman, to represent the interests opposed to approval of tax-exempt status for the two schools.

19. 461 U.S. 574 (1983), *aff'g*, 468 F. Supp. 890 (D.S.C. 1978), *rev'd*, 639 F.2d 147 (4th Cir. 1980). The decision also consolidated and affirmed the lower court's decision in Goldsboro Christian Schools, Inc. v. United States, 436 F. Supp. 1314 (E.D.N.C. 1977), *aff'd per curiam*, No. 80-1473 (4th Cir. Feb. 24, 1981)(unpublished opinion).

their religious beliefs. These beliefs, the Court found, cannot be accommodated with the government's compelling interest, and no "less restrictive means" are available to achieve the governmental interest.[20]

Bob Jones University offers schooling for 5,000 students from kindergarten through graduate school. It adheres to fundamentalist religious beliefs that include what might be charitably defined as judicially-diluted white supremacy. The University is absolutely opposed to interracial sex and marriage, and initially sought to enforce a prohibition on such unions within its community first by barring the enrollment of black students and then later by admitting only married black students.

Following a Fourth Circuit decision upholding an administrative ruling terminating all Veterans Administration assistance to the University due to its racially discriminatory admissions policy,[21] Bob Jones amended its admissions policy, and now permits unmarried black students to enroll. At the same time though, the school adopted a disciplinary rule providing that students who advocate or engage in interracial dating or marriage are subject to expulsion.[22]

Goldsboro Christian Schools has been more steadfast in its racially discriminatory policy and from its inception has absolutely prohibited the enrollment of black students. The Goldsboro school was opened in 1963 in evident response to the perceived need for a private, fundamentalist religious school that would "provide a private school education in a religious setting." The school has received financial support from and uses the facilities of the Second Baptist Church of Goldsboro, North Carolina.

Both schools argued that the Fourth Circuit erroneously applied the tax exemption provisions of the Internal Revenue Code. By requiring that they eschew all racial discrimination in the operation of their schools, they claimed infringement of their First Amendment rights to the free exercise of religion. In addition, they argued that the nondiscrimination requirement violated the establishment clause of the First Amendment by favoring religions that do not hold a religious belief opposing interracial dating and marriage.

In responding to these contentions, the Court noted that similar issues had earlier been decided against schools practicing racial discrimination, but *Green v. Connally*,[23] did not specifically reach the issue of whether the racial discrimination practiced by private religious schools is shielded by the free exercise or the establishment clauses from interference by the IRS regulations.

20. 103 S. Ct. at 2035.

21. Bob Jones University v. Johnson, 529 F.2d 514 (4th Cir. 1975). See also *Runyon v. McCrary*, 515 F.2d 1082 (4th Cir. 1975), *aff'd*, 427 U.S. 160 (1976).

22. Bob Jones University v. United States, 639 F.2d 147, 149 (4th Cir. 1980).

23. 330 F. Supp. 1150 (D.D.C. 1971), *aff'd mem. sub nom.*, Coit v. Green, 404 U.S. 997 (1971).

Chief Justice Burger's opinion dwelled on the major issue before the Supreme Court, the validity of withholding §501(c)(3) status to a private church school because of discriminatory racial policies mandated by religious beliefs. The opinion reviewed federal income tax law provisions which have long contained exemptions for certain charitable organizations, including the current Internal Revenue Code providing tax-exempt status for several charitable entities including those "operated exclusively for religious . . . or educational purposes . . ."[24]

"Charitable exemptions are justified," the Court found, "on the basis that the exempt entity confers a public benefit — a benefit which the society or the community may not itself choose or be able to provide, or which supplements and advances the work of public institutions already supported by tax revenues."[25] To warrant such exemption as provided by §501(c)(3), an institution must demonstrably serve and be in harmony with the public interest, and "must not be so at odds with the common community conscience as to undermine any public merit that might otherwise be conferred."[26]

The Court recognized the serious impact on an institution found not to be "charitable," but after reviewing the history of school segregation stated "there can no longer be any doubt that racial discrimination in education violates deeply and widely accepted views of elementary justice." The cases since *Brown*, the Court held, establish beyond doubt that "racial discrimination in education violates a most fundamental national policy, as well as rights of individuals." Citing a long list of actions by both Congress and the Executive intended to eliminate racial segregation, particularly in education, the Court concluded: "Whatever may be the rationale for such private schools' policies, and however sincere the rationale may be, racial discrimination in education is contrary to public policy."[27]

Finally, turning to the schools' claims that the IRS policy was invalid as to schools engaged in racial discrimination on the basis of sincerely held religious beliefs, the Court pointed out that the First Amendment's free exercise clause does not absolutely prohibit governmental regulation of religious beliefs. The state may justify a limitation on religious liberty by

24. I.R.C. §§501(a), (c)(3). Tax deductions are permitted for contributions to §501(c)(3) tax-exempt charitable organizations. I.R.C. §170(c).

25. 103 S. Ct. at 2029.

26. *Id.*

27. *Id.* at 2030. The Court rejected the contention by the petitioners, and indirectly that of the federal government, that only Congress could alter the scope of §§170 and 501(c)(3). The Internal Revenue Service had the authority to interpret these provisions and, given the strong actions by all three branches of government, it would have been anomalous for the IRS to blissfully ignore what the government had declared.

In this regard, the Court noted that Congress had not only failed to alter the IRS interpretation of the statutory provisions, but had rejected 13 bills introduced to overturn the IRS reading of §501(c)(3). *Id.* at 2033.

showing that it is essential to accomplish an overriding governmental interest. The governmental interest in ending racial discrimination is compelling and substantially outweighs whatever burden denial of tax benefits places on petitioners' exercise of their religious beliefs.[28]

The Court's decision in the *Bob Jones University* case enabled civil rights adherents to claim a hard-won victory. The opinion is sufficiently broad (too broad for Justice Powell's tastes) to end all reasonable speculation as to the proper balance in conflicts between the principles of racial justice and religious freedom. The Court did reach the First Amendment issues and affirmed the Fourth Circuit's decision in quite strong terms. Even so, civil rights adherents will have to ask once again whether they have won only another Pyrrhic victory. Consider:

— The serious undermining of school desegregation efforts occurred during the late 1960's and early 1970's; the litigation resulting in *Green v. Connally supra,* was intended to address this problem.

— Many of these schools that came to life as alternatives to school desegregation have long since faded from the scene. Those that survive with discriminatory policies in place have been maintained despite loss of their tax-exempt status.

— Few, if any, black parents are breaking down the doors and seeking admission for their children to schools like Bob Jones University.

Without underestimating the continuing danger, as well as the societal insult, posed for blacks by policies based on anti-miscegenation philosophies, it is at least worth speculating whether the time and resources focused on the Bob Jones University litigation might not have been more profitably devoted to providing educationally effective alternative schools to minority youngsters, all too many of whom are achieving no more impressively in nominally desegregated schools than their parents did in "separate but equal" school systems.

---

28. Justice Powell concurred in the decision, but questioned whether entitlement to tax-exempt status depends on organizations providing a clear "public benefit" as defined by the Court. *Id.* at 2037. He doubted that all or even most of the 106,000 organizations that filed §501(c)(3) tax returns in 1981 could demonstrate that they serve and are in harmony with the public interest. He also felt that the petitioners likely served the public interest through the substantially secular character of the curricula despite their racially discriminatory policies.

In this regard, he expressed concern about the "element of conformity" in the Court's analysis suggesting that tax-exempt entities must not act in a manner at odds with the declared position of the government. Such a view, Powell maintains, ignores the important role played by tax exemptions in encouraging diverse, and even sharply conflicting, activities and viewpoints. *Id.* at 2038.

Given the above, this author may be barred by espository estoppel from concurring with what the media called a significant defeat for the civil rights movement in the Court's decision in *Allen v. Wright.*[29] In a 5-3 ruling, the majority held that private citizens may not go to court to prod the federal government into denying or rescinding tax breaks for racially discriminatory schools.

The black parents who filed the suit charged that racially segregated private schools, with a total enrollment exceeding 750,000, enjoy tax-exempt status that is illegal under IRS policy affirmed in the *Bob Jones University* case, and directly harms their children's chances to receive a desegregated education. Justice O'Connor said people seeking more aggressive enforcement of the IRS policy should turn to Congress, not the federal courts, for help. Justice Brennan, in dissent, accused the Court of displaying "a startling insensitivity to the historical role played by the federal courts in eradicating race discrimination from our nation's schools."

While the controversy over barring religious-based schools that practice discrimination from receiving tax-exempt status has occupied the Supreme Court, determined private school forces have been attacked from an unexpected quarter. In *Fiedler v. Marumsco,*[30] a white father of a 14-year-old girl brought suit under Section 1981 and sought damages against a private, fundamentalist Christian school, operated by the church. The school had expelled the girl because of her "romantic relationship" with a black male classmate. The school has admitted blacks since 1972, but interprets the Bible as barring interracial dating, romance, and marriage. The district court cited the free exercise clause as its basis for dismissing the suit. The Fourth Circuit reversed.[31]

Reviewing the rationale of *Runyon v. McCrary,*[32] the court held that a commercially operated, private, sectarian school could not under Section 1981 discriminate on the basis of race in either its admissions or operating policies. Moreover, the church and school failed, in the court's view, to show that the pastor's actions, even if based on a religious rather than personal belief, were consistent with the church's beliefs. The church's position was not helped when it expelled the sister of the girl expelled for her interracial romance when the father contacted the NAACP after the first expulsion. The court found the sister's expulsion retaliatory and also barred by Section 1981.

29. 104 S. Ct. 3315 (1984).

30. 631 F.2d 1144 (4th Cir. 1980).

31. 486 F. Supp. 960 (E.D. Va. 1979). See summary in Second Edition, §3.11 n.1.

32. 392 U.S. 409 (1968). See Second Edition §3.10.

Chapter 3
Public Facilities: Symbols of Subordination

§3.6.1 *Public Accommodations Statutes*

Even hard-line critics of the civil rights movement are likely to concede that if the early years of protests accomplished anything, they achieved a breakdown of the system of segregation and exclusion of blacks from businesses open to the public. Laws have been passed, and the public generally assumes that such behavior is no longer acceptable. Yet racial discrimination in public places is still with us, often in quite blatant forms. The fact is, that despite the abolition of de jure segregation, and despite changed attitudes in a substantial portion of the populace, the desire of some whites to exercise dominance over blacks — even on the meanest grounds — remains strong.

To take just a few examples from the many cases reported in the past few years, black people are still suffering discrimination ranging from outright denial of service to grudging service or lower standards of service. A black business man agrees to rent an office and is later told that the office is unavailable;[1] a black customer is first insulted and then refused service when he challenges an increase in a price that he had checked over the phone;[2] black patrons are segregated on the second floor of a motel, and are discouraged from using the motel's recreational facilities;[3] a black man who tries to return his bus ticket for a refund is racially abused and accused of stealing the ticket;[4] a white woman with a black date is refused admission to a nightclub on the ground that she cannot produce proof of age, though she has offered four pieces of I.D.;[5] a black man is refused admission to a disco

1. Phiffer v. Proud Parrot Motor Hotel, Inc., 648 F.2d 548 (9th Cir. 1980).
2. Ledsinger v. Burmeister, 114 Mich. App. 12, 318 N.W.2d 558 (1982).
3. Director, Division on Civil Rights v. Slumber, Inc., 82 N.J. 412, 413 A.2d 603 (1980).
4. King v. Greyhound Lines, Inc., 61 Or. App. 197, 656 P.2d 349 (1982).
5. Gaudry v. Bureau of Labor and Industries, 48 Or. App. 589, 617 P.2d 668 (1980).

because of the dress code, though he can see that some white customers are dressed more casually than he;[6] yet another disco discourages black patronage by charging lower admission fees for whites.[7] These cases are at once shocking and mundane. They are unusual only in that complaints were actually filed and taken through the court system.

If the subject of public accommodations is no longer a high priority for civil rights crusaders, perhaps it is because all the battles have already been fought at least once, and seemingly adequate statutes have been enacted. We are now in the long, often painfully slow, process of using the existing law to modify ingrained social attitudes. This process can be accomplished only through prompt, effective enforcement of rights. The threat of legal penalties may not change the hearts of those who have been raised in prejudice, but it may modify their behavior, and it will reassure the victims of discrimination that society disapproves of such behavior.

The effectiveness of public accommodations statutes is often vitiated by small or token damage judgements for prevailing plaintiffs.[8] Because a purely moral victory is not generally sufficient motivation for the commitment of time and energy required to pursue a lawsuit, this discourages victims of discrimination from seeking legal solutions. Even with clients able to pay, many lawyers will not encourage litigation in an area of law with which they are unfamiliar and where a victory for a civil rights victim may alienate a host of potential business clients. Small judgements also indicate a lack of respect for the non-economic aspects of the damage suffered by those who are refused service or offered a lower grade of service in a public place.

As the Oregon Court of Appeals recognized in *King v. Greyhound Lines, Inc.*, the injury to an individual's sense of self-worth and personal integrity caused by discrimination in a public accommodation is a greater

6. McCuller v. Gaudry, 59 Or. App. 13, 650 P.2d 148 (1982).

7. McDaniel v. Cory, 631 P.2d 82 (Alaska 1981).

8. A typical award may include general damages, punitive damages, and attorneys fees. Judgments tend to fall between $1,000 to $2,000. See, Director, Division of Civil Rights v. Slumber, Inc., 82 N.J. 412, 413 A.2d 603 (1980)($1,500 to couple complaining of segregation in motel); King v. Greyhound Lines, Inc., 61 Or. App. 197, 656 P.2d 349 (1982)($500 general damages, $1,000 punitive damages and reasonable attorney's fees to man accused of stealing bus ticket presented for refund).

Plaintiffs who suffer economic losses seem to gain higher overall judgments, whereas plaintiffs who suffer only inconvenience or humiliation may receive nothing or a token award, despite favorable judgment on the discrimination issue. See Phiffer v. Proud Parrot Motor Hotel, Inc., 648 F.2d 548 (9th Cir. 1980)(insurance agent and wife who tried unsuccessfully to rent an office granted $7,500 general damages, $1,000 for emotional distress, $2,000 punitive damages and $2,500 in attorney's fees for a total of $13,000). *See also* McDaniel v. Cory, 631 P.2d 82 (Alaska 1981)(judgment of $600 for disco patron who was insulted and refused admission, settlement of $25 to another patron who did not press complaint; both judgments later overturned, see n.10 *infra.*).

evil than the monetary loss of a commercial transaction or the inconvenience of doing business elsewhere.[9] Though some courts recognize and compensate these injuries, there is no uniform method of calculating damages in public accommodations cases. The element of uncertainty as to the damages available even if the suit is successful is another factor that may discourage potential plaintiffs from pursuing public accommodations claims.

Though attorneys' fees are generally available (and this can be an important consideration in deciding whether to press a claim), defeat on a technicality can prevent attorneys from being compensated. Such a situation arose in *McDaniel v. Cory* [10] where the Alaska Supreme Court held that the Alaska State Commission for Human Rights did not have the power to award compensatory damages to complainants.[11] Though the court upheld the Commission's finding that the defendant's disco was operated in a racially discriminatory manner, the issue on appeal was the Commission's power to award damages. Since the plaintiffs lost on that issue, no attorneys' fees could be awarded.

Further difficulties are caused by the sheer number of statutes on the books. The confusing abundance of federal, state, and administrative (both federal and state) remedies sometimes causes plaintiffs to lose, not because they do not have a good case but because they filed under the wrong statute.[12] The response of plaintiffs' attorneys is to become overly cautious, and to burden the courts by pleading every conceivable statutory or common law claim.[13] An increasing proportion of public accommodations claims seem to originate and be resolved under state statutes,[14] perhaps because state public accommodations laws do not offer the daunting variety of

9. King v. Greyhound Lines, Inc., 61 Or. App. 197, 203, 656 P.2d 349, 352 (1982). (See Chapter 8 for further discussion of emotional distress resulting from acts of discrimination.)

10. McDaniel v. Cory, 631 P.2d 82 (Alaska 1981).

11. No unanimity exists among the various states as to the remedies that may be granted in administrative proceedings. In contrast to *McDaniel*, the New Jersey Supreme Court has specifically held that the state Division on Civil Rights may grant damages to nonparty complainants in its hearings on public accommodations offenses. Director, Division on Civil Rights v. Slumber, Inc., 82 N.J. 412, 413 A.2d 603 (1980).

12. *See, e.g.*, Human Rights Commission of New Mexico v. Board of Regents of the University of New Mexico College of Nursing, 95 N.M. 576, 624 P.2d 518 (1981)(claim of racial and sexual discrimination in treatment of students; filed under Title II, should have been filed under Title IV).

13. In Ledsinger v. Burmeister, 114 Mich. App. 12, 318 N.W.2d 558 (1982) plaintiffs sued a merchant who shouted racial epithets at Mr. Ledsinger under 42 U.S.C. §1983, two Michigan civil rights statutes, and common law theories of slander, publication of embarrassing private facts, intentional infliction of emotional distress, and loss of consortium.

14. Speaking with no statistical backup, about twice as many state as federal cases seem to have reached the appellate level since 1980.

federal civil rights statutes, and because plaintiffs hope that state courts will be faster and less crowded than federal. Many of the reported state law claims originate in agency proceedings, and we may assume that a larger number of unreported cases are dealt with successfully at the administrative stage.

§3.6.2 Government Services and Facilities

Most public accommodations statutes, whether state or federal, are aimed at private entities offering goods or services to the public. Government services, such as education, are not covered by Title II or by state public accommodations laws.[15] Moreover, public accommodations statutes are really designed to furnish remedies for individuals experiencing acts of discrimination, rather than the large classes of people affected when public officials discriminate. However, minority individuals or groups suffering from discrimination in provision of government facilities or services may have a constitutional claim or a right of action under one of many federal statutes: 42 U.S.C. §§1981 or 1983, Title VI (barring discrimination in programs receiving federal funds), the Revenue Sharing Act, the Housing and Urban Development Act. The difficulty, as always, is in judging which provision to use, and in presenting a set of facts and arguments that compel a legal remedy.

The cities and towns of America, both north and south, still reflect the historical realities of segregation. As James Kushner notes in his recent guide to fair housing law, the classic phrase "wrong side of the tracks" continues to accurately describe the tendency of minority neighborhoods to lack the quality of services taken for granted in white neighborhoods.[16] Though systematic discrimination in the provision of municipal services violates the Fourteenth Amendment,[17] a walk across the railroad tracks in many towns still takes one from a community with paved roads, street lights, carefully maintained parks, and modern water, sewer, and drainage service to an area where many roads are little more than unpaved alleys, parks are more like vacant lots than "recreational facilities," drainage is

15. *See, e.g.*, Human Rights Commission of New Mexico v. Board of Regents of the University of New Mexico School of Nursing, 95 N.M. 576, 624 P.2d 518 (1981)(state-run college not a public accommodation; complaint dismissed despite finding of racial discrimination).

16. Kushner, *Fair Housing: Discrimination in Real Estate, Community Development and Revitalization* 322 (1983).

17. Hawkins v. Town of Shaw, 437 F.2d 1286 (5th Cir. 1971) *aff'd en banc*, 461 F.2d 1171 (5th Cir. 1972)(97 percent of the town's unpaved streets were in the black community, no high-power mercury vapor lights had been installed in the area, parts of the black community had no sewer system, and had open ditches for a drainage system).

provided by open ditches, and water and sewer connections may never have been installed.

In two cases recently decided in Florida, *Johnson v. City of Arcadia*[18] and *Dowdell v. City of Apopka*,[19] the Eleventh Circuit found conditions equaling or exceeding those just described and held that city officials had intentionally discriminated in the provision of municipal services, violating the Fourteenth Amendment and Title VI.[20] Both towns were established in the late nineteenth century and developed under strict de jure segregation; in Apopka, the segregation laws were not repealed until 1968.[21]

Arcadia had a population of 7,000, about 32 percent black, when suit was filed in 1976. At that time all black residents lived in an area bordered by railroad tracks and distinguished by the poor condition of its homes, the high proportion of unpaved roads, and inadequate water and sewer service. Recreational facilities in the white and black areas provided a striking contrast: the community center on the white side of town was extensive, fully equipped, and well maintained; the community center in the black neighborhood was a one room basketball gym that could be reached only by crossing an unbridged ditch.[22]

For many years city officials had ignored complaints from the black community, and refused to act upon a consulting firm's report that the black area was severely blighted and should receive priority in allocations of city funds. The consulting firm noted in its report that while not all sections of the white community had complete and up-to-date facilities, whatever funds were available had clearly gone only into white areas.[23] The court found that the dramatic inequalities in services and facilities provided by the city to black and white residents were the result of systematic racial discrimination, and included in its order a plan to distribute federal revenue sharing funds so as to upgrade facilities in the black community.

The conditions in Apopka, Florida were very similar. Apopka is a town of 5,000, about 30 percent black. All but a few of its black residents live in a neighborhood on the southwest side of the highway and railroad tracks. Most city officials and employees are white. Though nearly $800,000 had been spent in the 1970's to extend municipal services to newly annexed white neighborhoods, the black community still had many unpaved and dead-end roads, no storm water drainage system, undersized and insufficient water mains, and unconnected sewer lines.[24] Black residents began a complaint campaign, and when city officials refused to act, initiated

18. Johnson v. City of Arcadia, 450 F. Supp. 1363 (M.D. Fla. 1978).

19. Dowdell v. City of Apopka, 511 F. Supp. 1375 (M.D. Fla. 1981), *modified*, 698 F.2d 1181 (11th Cir. 1983).

20. 42 U.S.C.A. §2000d (1983).

21. 511 F. Supp. at 1379.

22. 450 F. Supp. at 1368.

23. *Id.* at 1370.

24. 511 F. Supp. at 1378.

this suit. The court found that the inferior services provided to the black community constituted intentional discrimination under the Fourteenth Amendment, Title VI, and the Revenue Sharing Act.[25] Using the *Arcadia* case as its precedent, the district court enjoined the City of Apopka from spending any revenue sharing funds to construct or improve any municipal facilities in white areas until services and facilities in the black community were brought up to par. On appeal, the Eleventh Circuit upheld the injunction but remanded on the issue of whether the city's litigation and settlement expenses could be reimbursed through taxes.[26]

Cases such as these would seem to be powerful precedents, but their influence is limited by other developments in civil rights law.[27] First, under *Washington v. Davis* the violation must be demonstrated by proof of intent and not just by discriminatory impact.[28] In the absence of published statements proclaiming city officials' intention to discriminate, intent is most easily proved in small towns with a clear history of segregation. In large urban areas measurement of service delivery is difficult, and officials can simply argue that the limited funds available have been allocated on a rational basis and that inequities in services are a product of economic forces rather than prejudice.

Secondly, even when discriminatory intent is apparent, plaintiffs may have difficulty proving that they have received unequal services. Under *Beal v. Lindsay*, the measure of comparability of services is input, not results.[29] Because a greater investment may be needed to maintain services and facilities in poorer communities, especially where theft and vandalism are prevalent, an equal allocation of funds may result in deterioration. Similarly, a funding system based on extent of use may result in shrinking budgets for facilities that cannot be fully used because they are already rundown, poorly equipped, and inadequately staffed. Such systems, though based on a seemingly neutral standard, tend to result in the improvement of well-maintained facilities, and the deterioration of poorer ones.[30]

Finally, precedents like *Arcadia*, *Apopka* or *Hawkins v. Town of Shaw*[31] are not applicable when services are financed by special assessment of property owners rather than citywide taxes. The courts have consistently held that there is no constitutional violation when such plans are offered on equal terms, despite the fact that only affluent neighborhoods can afford the

25. The State and Local Assistance Act of 1972, 31 U.S.C. §12 (1982).

26. 698 F.2d at 1184.

27. This discussion owes a large debt to James Kushner's analysis of municipal services in *Fair Housing: Discrimination in Real Estate, Community Development and Revitalization*, 321-326 (1983).

28. Washington v. Davis, 426 U.S. 289 (1976).

29. Beal v. Lindsay, 468 F.2d 287 (2d Cir. 1972).

30. Kushner, *supra* note 27, at 322.

31. Hawkins v. Town of Shaw, 437 F.2d 1286 (5th Cir. 1971), *aff'd en banc*, 461 F.2d 1171 (5th Cir. 1972).

assessments.[32] The courts have not directly addressed the underlying issue of whether there is any fundamental right to receive municipal services.

Issues concerning municipal services are rarely as clear-cut in large urban areas as in small towns. The misery in our inner cities is caused by a combination of forces, including racial prejudice, but impersonal economic and social trends are also factors. Whatever the causes, it is not disputed that blacks and other minorities constitute a disproportionate percentage of inner city dwellers. The difficulty comes when urban officials must balance the competing claims of many interest groups for limited city funds. Somehow, though city officials may have the best intentions, the interests of minorities rarely seem to weigh as heavily as those of other groups. The recent spate of cases challenging the closure or relocation of inner city hospitals illustrates the difficulties minority groups face in challenging municipal decisions that adversely affect them.

Though closing and relocation of hospitals is a continuous process, reflecting population change and growth, and the age and condition of structures, closings and relocations over the past 40 years have affected black neighborhoods disproportionately.[33] In part, this is the result of two trends: first, the financial difficulties brought on when the income level of a hospital's clientele drops, and second, a shortage of physicians caused by the tendency of physicians to follow well-heeled patients out to the suburbs. Difficulties such as an old or inadequate building become decisive only when the hospital lacks resources to remodel and update.[34] When a hospital in an inner city neighborhood is closed, it leaves a vacuum; the few individual practitioners in the area often depart, established relationships with patients are broken, and residents faced with a cross-town journey to the nearest health facility often substitute emergency treatment for preventative care.[35] Hospitals also serve other community functions, as large em-

32. *See, e.g.*, Citizens for Underground Equality v. City of Seattle, 6 Wash. App. 338, 492 P.2d 1071 (1972) (residents of low-income neighborhood opposed plan to fund installation of underground utility lines through assessment of property owners. The court held that though some sections of the city might be unable or unwilling to pay such assessments, the plan was constitutional).

33. "Urban Hospital Closings in the Face of Racial Change, a statement on Hospital Financing Problems to the Sub-committee on Health, Committee on Ways and Means, U.S. House of Representatives, March 14, 1980," by Alan Sager, Ph.D., Assistant Professor of Urban and Health Planning, Brandeis University. Reprinted in *Civil Rights Issues in Health Care Delivery*, (a consultation sponsored by the United States Commission on Civil Rights), Washington, D.C., April 15-16, 1980, p. 383.

Id. at 388: "As the minority proportion of the neighborhood increases, so does the proportion of hospitals closing or relocating from 1937 to 1977. In neighborhoods 0-25 percent black in 1970, for example, only 14.1 percent of the 1937 hospitals had closed or relocated by 1977. But in neighborhoods 76-100 percent black in 1970, fully 46.9 percent of hospitals — almost half — had disappeared."

34. *Id.* at 395.

35. *Id.* at 396.

ployers and symbols of neighborhood identity, that may not be replaced when the hospital leaves.

To prevent such consequences, minority and low-income interest groups in Wilmington, Delaware filed suit challenging plans to reorganize the Delaware Medical Center so that 75 percent of its beds and many services would be available only at a new suburban hospital.[36] The medical center was comprised of three central city hospitals, all in financial trouble, partly because of the high proportion of free service provided to low-income patients. Due to its old and inadequate buildings, the Medical Center was in danger of losing medical school accreditation in numerous specialties. After minority groups began to protest the reorganization plan, HEW intervened and negotiated minor revisions in the plan, including free shuttle service between the facilities, pregnancy care for teenage mothers and other services designed to improve health care for minority residents.[37]

The district court held that the hospital had shown sufficient basis for adoption of the revised plan to overcome a prima facie showing of disparate impact on minority and low-income people. The Third Circuit affirmed, noting that the plaintiffs had not established facts to show that an alternate plan, such as splitting beds and services equally between the facilities or leaving the majority of beds in the city, would be more feasible or less expensive.[38] Conceding that the burdens of travel to and from the suburban facility will fall on minorities and low-income city dwellers, the court seemed to feel that no more accommodation to these groups' needs could be expected.

Similar suits were filed in New York City and St. Louis, with comparable results. In *Bryan v. Koch*[39] the Second Circuit found no showing of discriminatory intent in the closure of Harlem's Sydenham Hospital, and held that the use of criteria such as age, obsolescence, cost overruns, and proximity of other facilities provided a legitimate basis for the choice of which hospital to close that was sufficient to overcome a prima facie showing of disparate impact upon minorities. To plaintiff's contention that the city should have considered alternative plans, the court replied that Title VI does not require consideration of alternatives beyond a rational assessment of all hospitals in the system, noting that courts should be wary of substituting their judgement for that of government officials.[40] In *Jackson v. Conway*[41] the closure of the Homer G. Phillips Hospital on the north side of St. Louis was upheld despite a showing that minority patients would be dispro-

36. NAACP v. The Medical Center, Inc., 657 F.2d 1322 (3d Cir. 1981), *aff'g*, 491 F. Supp 290 (D. Del. 1980).

37. *Id.* at 1331.

38. *Id.* at 1335.

39. 627 F.2d 612 (2d Cir. 1980) *aff'g*, 492 F. Supp. 212 (S.D.N.Y. 1980).

40. *Id.* at 619.

41. Jackson v. Conway, 620 F.2d 680 (8th Cir. 1980), *aff'g*, 476 F. Supp. 896 (E.D. Mo. 1979).

portionately inconvenienced by the closure, because projections showed that the overall quality of health care in the city would be improved.

§3.7.1 The Private Club Exemption

Private clubs continue to occupy an anomalous position in the scheme of public accommodations laws. Though private clubs are exempted from Title II,[42] and in most cases under §1981, to this date no federal court has found a defendant organization to be truly private. The waters are further muddied by the Supreme Court's failure to develop standards for identifying what would qualify as a truly private club. With the state of the law so uncertain, organizations feel little pressure to change discriminatory membership policies until forced to do so by legal action.

There seems little chance of legislative action to amend Title II, either to abolish the private club exemption or to distinguish between private social clubs and organizations that are largely adjuncts of the marketplace. The American Bar Association recently approved a recommendation urging Congress to amend Title II to include in the definition of public accommodation private clubs that derive substantial income from business sources.[43] Such a proposal would not affect clubs primarily devoted to social or charitable activities, only clubs whose main function is to provide business-related facilities and services. This would include clubs where a substantial portion of club dues are provided by businesses and employers and where revenues are derived from providing conference rooms, and food and beverage service for business meetings.[44] However, since these

42. 42 U.S.C.A. §2000a(e) (1983).

43. Recommendation to the ABA House of Delegates, approved August 2, 1983:

> BE IT RESOLVED, That the American Bar Association endorses amendments to Title II of the Civil Rights Act of 1964, 42 U.S.C. §2000a (which prohibits discrimination in public accommodations on the basis of race, color, religion, or national origin) to:
> (1) include in the definition of the term "public accommodation" any private club or other establishment which derives a substantial portion of its income from business sources;
> (2) provide an adequate objective standard by which to measure "a substantial portion of income from business sources."

The ABA action, however, must be viewed in the context of its failure, during the same session, to pass an amendment to Canon 2A of the Code of Judicial Conduct requiring judges to refrain from membership in private clubs that engage in invidious discrimination.

44. The ABA report supporting its proposal to amend Title II concluded (p. 4-5) that many private clubs are essentially extensions of the marketplace, organized to promote business purposes, and funded by dues provided by business and employers.

business oriented clubs have impressive lobbying powers, and since Congressional ardor for civil rights has noticeably cooled, even such a limited amendment would be unlikely to succeed.

Much of the confusion generated by the private club exemption could be dissipated by judicial explication of just what it is that makes a club private. Though federal courts continue to find that challenged clubs are not truly private,[45] this is a case by case process that has not provided a working, predictive definition for plaintiffs and attorneys. Though we may suspect it, we cannot be sure that no truly private clubs actually exist. At the very least a judicial definition should follow the lines of the ABA proposal and weed out business supported clubs from the ranks of so-called private clubs.

And a judicial ruling will likely be needed. In *Perkins v. New Orleans Athletic Club*,[46] the court found that private clubs that do not serve as vital a community role as schools, could be characterized as closed, exclusive, independent, private organizations. And even if they admitted all whites "who are middle class, non-black, male, and apt to pay their bills," the club is not covered in the seemingly all-inclusive language of 42 U.S.C. §1981.[47] In that opinion, the court noted that the Club was losing money, suggesting that eventually financial pressures might overcome the tradition of barring blacks that dates back to its opening in 1872. The hope was premature.

In a vote taken in early July 1984, Club members voted 161 to 124 to maintain their whites-only policy. Proponents of change urged that admitting blacks would bring in more money, and were encouraged that the vote was closer than when the issue went to a ballot in 1976, at the time of the *Perkins* case, when the integration proposal lost by an 8-to-1 margin.[48]

In recent years women's groups have seized the initiative in private club challenges, focusing particularly on clubs with a business orientation. Though an increasing number of women are being hired for management-level positions, many find that further advancement is difficult without access to the private clubs where executives congregate. A surprising number of clubs that provide business facilities such as meeting rooms and convention services, as well as social facilities, refuse to admit women or grant women only limited membership.

45. *See, e.g.*, Wright v. The Salisbury Club, Ltd., 632 F.2d 309 (4th Cir. 1980), holding that a club offering sports and dining facilities to all residents of a subdivision, as well as some nonresidents, was not a truly private club under Title II. The court found that the club rejected the membership application of a black couple who had moved into the subdivision solely on the basis of their race. The court also held that club membership was a property right granted to all purchasers of subdivision lots, and that refusing the use of club facilities to the Wrights violated §1982.

46. 429 F. Supp. 661 (E.D. La. 1976). The case is discussed in some detail in the Second Edition, §3.10, text at nn.7-11.

47. Unreported opinion of May 19, 1976 at 4-5.

48. N.Y. Times, July 9, 1984, at 7, col. 7.

A typical example is the Petroleum Club of Lafayette, Louisiana, a center for petroleum industry business meetings and conferences. The club allows women only in certain dining rooms during limited hours, and will not admit even female employees of member corporations to its meeting rooms.[49] These practices were upheld in *Whitten v. Petroleum Club of Lafayette*, despite the court's recognition that a great deal of business is done at the club and that exclusion handicaps women's careers.[50]

While women and blacks are natural allies in challenging such practices, their legal positions, and consequently their legal strategies, differ. Though some state public accommodations statutes prohibit discrimination on the basis of sex, women are not covered by Title II,[51] and so have minimal interest in challenging the private club exemption. Attacks based on other federal statutes or the Constitution have not succeeded so far, but seem to hold the greatest potential for women's groups. Of course, if women find a constitutional or statutory rationale to break down private club barriers, blacks and other minorities will benefit.

At long last, the Supreme Court has become involved in *Roberts v. United States Jaycees*,[52] a case raising the conflict between Minnesota's efforts to eliminate sex-based discrimination against its citizens and the constitutional right of freedom of association asserted by members of a private organization. The Jaycees club is organized largely to promote business and to advance the business careers of its members. Women may become associate but not full members, and may not run for club offices, vote, or compete for achievement awards, though they may participate in activities for which such awards are given.

This controversy arose when a Minnesota chapter of the Jaycees began admitting women as full members after the Minnesota Supreme Court ruled that state public accommodations statutes applied to such clubs.[53] The national Jaycees organization sanctioned the Minnesota chapter and ordered it to discontinue this practice. The local chapter filed suit against the U.S. Jaycees and won a ruling prohibiting the national organization from disciplining a chapter for its compliance with state law. The district court emphasized that the Minnesota statute was aimed at economic discrimination rather than purely social clubs.[54]

On appeal, however, the Eighth Circuit held that the Minnesota statute was unconstitutional because it violated the Jaycees' associational right to

49. Whitten v. Petroleum Club of Lafayette, 508 F. Supp. 765, 767 (W.D. La. 1981).

50. *Id.* at 767.

51. *Id.* at 772. The *Whitten* court also rejected plaintiff's claims under §1983 (no state action), §1985(3) (a single corporate entity cannot conspire with itself) and Title VII (the club was not the woman's employer).

52. 104 S. Ct. 3244 (1984), *rev'g* 709 F.2d 1560 (8th Cir. 1983).

53. United States Jaycees v. McClure, 305 N.W.2d 764 (Minn. 1981).

54. United States Jaycees v. McClure, 534 F. Supp. 766 (D. Minn. 1982).

limit their contacts with women.[55] Moreover, it held that since the statute supplies no standard for the definition of organizations as "business oriented" or "private" it was void for vagueness. In his dissent from the denial of rehearing, Judge Heaney argued cogently that though "young men have the right to associate with whomever they please," young women who are excluded from a business oriented organization are deprived of equal opportunity to compete for leadership positions in society.[56]

The comment proved prophetic. Justice Brennan found that Minnesota has a compelling state interest in eradicating discrimination against its female citizens, thereby protecting them from a number of serious social and personal harms. Making a distinction between freedom of intimate association (e.g., creation and sustenance of a family, marriage, childbirth, raising and education of children), and freedom of expressive association, (e.g., collective effort toward shared goals), he found the Jaycees' outside of the category of highly personal relaionships entitled to constitutional protection against unjustified interference by the state.

While acknowledging that Minnesota's law may interfere with the Jaycees' rights of expressive association, it must also be acknowledged that the statute is unrelated to the suppression of expression and the impact its application may have on male Jaycees' freedom of expressive association is justified. Brennan said the Court declined to indulge in the sexual stereotyping that underlay the Jaycees' contentions that, by allowing women in the organization to vote, the Minnesota law will change the content or impact of the group's speech. He also found no basis in the record for charges that admission of women as full voting members will impede the Jaycees' ability to engage in constitutionally protected civic, charitable, lobbying, fundraising, and other activities or to disseminate its preferred views. And, he added, even if enforcement of the Act causes some incidental abridgment of Jaycees' protected speech, that effect is not greater than necessary to accomplish the state's legitimate purposes.

The next step, of course, is to extend the ruling in the *Jaycees* case to jurisdictions with less supportive state civil rights laws. Justice Brennan's opinion laid a strong foundation for reaching such a conclusion on strictly constitutional grounds, but ominously for such a result, Justices Rehnquist and O'Connor concurred in only the judgment, and O'Connor in a separate concurring opinion, parted company with the Court over its First Amendment analysis which, in her view, "adopted a test that unadvisedly casts doubt on the power of States to pursue the profoundly important goal of ensuring nondiscriminatory access to commercial opportunities in our society. At the same time, the Court has adopted an approach to the general problem presented by this case that accords insufficient protection to ex-

55. 709 F.2d at 1578.
56. Eighth Circuit Slip Opinion, August 1, 1983.

pressive associations and places inappropriate burdens on groups claiming the protection of the First Amendment."[57]

57. 104 S. Ct. at 3257. It is not clear whether Justice O'Connor's concerns included a fear that the Jaycees' 12-year, one million dollar legal fight to bar women from full membership, would collapse under the burden of the Supreme Court's decision. In any event, six weeks after that decision, a special meeting of Jaycee delegates voted 5,372 to 386 to admit women. One official, explaining the action, said the Supreme Court's ruling in the Minnesota case left the Jaycees "no choice" but to admit women. The Oregonian, Aug. 17, 1984, at A1, col. 4.

Part II
Stages of Citizenship Suppression

Chapter 4
Voting Rights and Democratic Domination

§4.1 *Introduction: 1984*

Early in his candidacy for the Democratic Party's presidential nomination, the Reverend Jesse Jackson told a reporter: "The truth is that blacks will no longer be the Harlem Globetrotters of the Democratic Party. We will no longer provide the excitement, tricks and music while white males assume the position of proprietorship."[1]

While (with good reason) the attention of civil rights advocates has been centered on discriminatory voting policies and the resulting dilution of black political power, too little concern has been voiced about the treatment of blacks by the political party that, since the days of the depression and Franklin Delano Roosevelt, has benefited from the staunch support of most black voters.[2] In his typically colorful statement, Jackson identifies the subsidiary role the Democratic Party has long set aside for blacks, particularly at the national level.

As this is written, it appears that Democratic Party leaders are willing to jeopardize their slim chances of ousting President Reagan by treating Jackson and his campaign as though it was the enemy rather than the source of literally millions of new Democratic votes. It is not hard to predict a major increase in black political participation if Democrats move to meet the desire of blacks for a meaningful role in party policymaking. Jackson has shown that without a major campaign chest or the endorsement of major interests, a black candidate willing to depart from traditional campaign

1. *Is the U.S. Ready for a Black President?* U.S. News & World Report, 21-22 (July 25, 1983).

2. One writer reports, "Blacks have been the party's most consistent constituency, casting 20 to 22 percent of the Democratic vote total in the last four Presidential elections — making them more loyal than Jews, ethnic Catholics, Hispanics or Southern whites." Delaney, "Voting: The New Black Power," N.Y. Times, Nov. 27, 1983, §6 (Magazine), at 35, 52.

activity and rhetoric can not only galvanize impressive numbers of black and other minority voters, but generate some white support as well.

Strangely, many black Democratic officeholders seem reluctant to accept this. Black mayors, who themselves gained office by defying conventional political wisdom, are supporting the Democratic Party front-runner, Walter Mondale, justifying their choice on the traditional truism that "Jesse, as a black, can't win." But Jackson's campaign has survived, though several white candidates called it quits. This is a fact hard to ignore, particularly when it is considered along with the impact of increased political participation by blacks, which in recent years has resulted in a substantial increase in the number of black elected officials — from 1,469 in 1970 to 5,606 in 1983.[3]

Another indicator is the number of major cities with black mayors: Atlanta, Chicago, Los Angeles, Newark, Philadelphia, and San Antonio has a Hispanic mayor. Most important of all is the revolutionary breakthrough of the Jesse Jackson campaign proving that even at the national level, blacks need not subordinate their legitimate aspirations to the racially subordinating strategies of white party leaders.

There remains a real concern that the twentieth century civil rights gains in voting, like those achieved in the nineteenth century, will not survive the country's current conservative era. But as political scientist Dianne M. Pinderhughes[4] points out, significant changes have occurred which may preclude or at least reduce the possibility of a return to the status quo. The Congress has continued to legislate surprisingly strong federal protection for voting rights, and the new laws have been upheld by the Supreme Court, which itself has broadened its definition of the constitutionally protected, "one person, one vote" doctrine to include the dilution of voting strength via politically motivated gerrymandering of district lines. This judicial movement could substantially enhance the growing black voting strength in state and local elections.[5]

The euphoria in the black community over the realization that a black person can run as a serious presidential candidate, and the political power resident in that potential, is sobered by the hostility the Jackson campaign has encountered from much of the American Establishment. How shall we read that hostility? The bookkeeping of his Operation PUSH is subjected to scrutiny far more intense than that given to Presidential counselor, Edwin Meese. Jackson is pushed hard to condemn the statements of Minister Louis Farrakhan, but no such pressure is mounted against those in extremist Jewish groups who have threatened, and carried out, violent acts against

3. 70 ABA J. 52 (1984).

4. Pinderhughes, *The Black Vote — The Sleeping Giant* in The State of Black America 1984 69 (1984).

5. See discussion, *infra* at §4.15.1.

the Jackson campaign to underscore their opposition to Jackson's support of a homeland for the Palestinians.

The response of the Democratic Party to the Jackson campaign could prove critical to the party's success both in the 1984 Presidential elections and for years to come. It is quite clear that Jackson has the support of a large percentage of the black voting population. His positions accurately reflect their interests and concerns. Embracing wholeheartedly those interests and concerns will be difficult for a party that, despite the faithful support of its black minority, must be concerned for the viewpoint of the voting majority that they fear, not without justification, is not ready for a black President, particularly one who espouses the interests and concerns of blacks and other dispossessed Americans.

For decades the Democratic Party has relied on the political fact that blacks have no place else to go. But undue reliance on the "no alternatives" strategy by Party leaders could court political suicide if blacks are ready to carry through on Jesse Jackson's warning that "blacks will no longer be the Harlem Globetrotters of the Democratic Party."

§4.5.1 The City of Mobile Solution, Undone

Perhaps still enthralled with the notion that the intent standard of *Washington v. Davis*[6] was an appropriate means of balancing the interests of racial equality advocates with those urging the retention of the political-economic status quo, the Court seriously undermined the carefully wrought *Zimmer* standards[7] in *City of Mobile v. Bolden.*[8]

In *Bolden*, a plurality of the Supreme Court found that Section 2 of the Voting Rights Act of 1965,[9] did not authorize judicial relief in vote dilution cases in the absence of proof that the alleged discrimination was intentionally imposed. In their view, Section 2 was intended to have an effect no different than that of the Fifteenth Amendment, and the Fifteenth Amendment bars only direct, purposeful denial or abridgment of the right of blacks to cast a ballot. Vote dilution claims are cognizable solely under the Fourteenth Amendment, and require proof of a purpose or intent to discriminate in their adoption to entitle plaintiffs to relief. The Court remanded the case for a determination of whether Mobile's at-large election system for its city commissioners was adopted or maintained with a discriminatory purpose. The imposition of an intent requirement that could not be met by application of indirect proof via the *Zimmer* standards repre-

6. 426 U.S. 229 (1976).

7. Zimmer v. McKeithen, 485 F.2d 1297 (5th Cir. 1973).

8. 446 U.S. 55 (1980). The lower court decision is summarized in the Second Edition at §4.13, text at n.14.

9. 42 U.S.C. §§1971, 1973-1973p (1981).

sented a dramatic change from pre-*Bolden* cases under the Voting Rights Act, and the case received a great deal of comment.[10]

On remand, civil rights lawyers, determining that the dilution of black voters in Mobile was hardly fortuitous, retained historians whose testimony convinced the district court that the history of de jure segregation and discrimination in Mobile supported the inference that the at-large voting system had been instituted with discriminatory intent.[11]

Plaintiffs commissioned historians, including Professor J. Morgan Kousser,[12] to review the motivating circumstances under which Mobile's at-large electoral system was established at the turn of the century. They found it was adopted in principal part to discriminate against blacks and deny them access to the political process and elective office. To support this finding, the experts presented a historical pattern of denying the ballot to blacks stretching back to the early 1800's, with the exception of the Reconstruction era, and the record of violence and intimidation against blacks during that period is set out in gory detail.

During the Redemption period in the 1870's, whites decided on at-large elections in Mobile for the first time since 1828 to exclude blacks from office. They were not opposed to blacks voting, but moderate and conservative Republicans and Democrats shared the view that only whites should hold office. No blacks have been elected since. Ward elections were restored as to primary elections where blacks were excluded under state law. Later in 1876, the state legislature repealed all provisions providing for minority representation. When state law in 1909 required redistricting, Mobile adopted a city commission form of government that enabled them to maintain at-large voting. They saw this as the best means to keep blacks from holding office — in case they were reinfranchised by federal intervention.

Based on the historical evidence, the court reversed its earlier finding that the 1911 change did not affect blacks because they were already barred by the 1901 Constitutional change. It found, moreover, that the effects of century-old discriminatory intent continued to the present, in violation of both the Voting Rights Act and the Fourteenth and Fifteenth Amendments.[13]

10. *See, e.g,* Comment, *City of Mobile v. Bolden: A Setback in the Fight Against Discrimination*, 47 Brooklyn L. Rev. 169 (1980); Comment, *The Standard of Proof in At-Large Vote Dilution Discrimination Cases After City of Mobile v. Bolden*, 10 Fordham Urb. L.J. 103 (1981); Note, *City of Mobile v. Bolden: Voter Dilution and the New Intent Requirements Under the Fifteenth and Fourteenth Amendments*, 18 Hous. L. Rev. 611 (1981); and Comment, *City of Mobile v. Bolden: The Uncertain Future of Racial Vote Dilution*, 25 St. Louis U.L.J. 657 (1981).

11. Bolden v. City of Mobile Alabama, 542 F. Supp. 1050 (S.D. Ala. 1982).

12. Professor Kousser's work, The Shaping of Southern Politics (1974), is cited in the Second Edition, §4.3 nn.2-4, 6.

13. This result was affirmed in Brown v. Board of School Commrs. of Mobile County, 706 F.2d 1103 (11th Cir. 1983).

§4.5.2 The Voting Rights Act: 1982 Legislation

Soon after the Supreme Court announced the *Bolden* decision, civil rights groups began lobbying Congress to consider amending Section 2 of the Voting Rights Act, which provides a private right of action to challenge state practices that affect minority voting power.[14] After lengthy consideration Congress approved amendments clarifying whether proof of discriminatory intent or purpose is necessary to establish a violation of Section 2.[15]

The revised version of Section 2 resurrects the principles applied in voting cases prior to *Bolden*. Plaintiffs who are able to show denial of opportunity to participate in the electoral process on an equal basis need not prove discriminatory intent. The Report of the Senate Committee on the Judiciary states:

> In pre-*Bolden* cases plaintiffs could prevail by showing that a challenged election law or procedure, in the context of the total circumstances of the local election process, had the result of denying a racial or language minority an equal chance to participate in the electoral process. Under this results test, it was not necessary to demonstrate that the challenged election law or procedure was designed or maintained for a discriminatory purpose.
>
> In *Bolden*, a plurality of the Supreme Court broke with precedent and substantially increased the burden on plaintiffs in voting discrimination cases by requiring proof of discriminatory purpose. The Com-

14. The original §2, provided that:

> No voting qualification or prerequisite to voting, or standard, practice, or procedure shall be imposed or applied by any State or political subdivision to deny or abridge the right of any citizen of the United States to vote on account of race or color, or in contravention of the guarantees set forth in section 1973b(f)(2) of this title. 42 U.S.C. §1973 (1976).

15. Section 2 of the Voting Rights Act of 1965, 42 U.S.C. §1973 (1982), 42 U.S.C.A. §1973b (Supp. 1983), provides:

> (a) No voting qualification or prerequisite to voting or standard, practice, or procedure shall be imposed or applied by any State or political subdivision in a manner which results in a denial or abridgment of the right of any citizen of the United States to vote on account of race or color, or in contravention of the guarantees set forth in §4(f)(2) [42 U.S.C. §1973(f)(2)], as provided in subsection (b).
> (b) A violation of subsection (a) is established if, based on the totality of circumstances, it is shown that the political processes leading to nomination or election in the State or political subdivision are not equally open to participation by members of a class of citizens protected by subsection (a) in that its members have less opportunity than other members of the electorate to participate in the political process and to elect representatives of their choice. The extent to which members of a protected class have been elected to office in the State or political subdivision is one circumstance which may be considered: *Provided*, That nothing in this section establishes a right to have members of a protected class elected in numbers equal to their proportion in the population.

> mittee has concluded that this intent test places an unacceptably difficult burden on plaintiffs. It diverts the judicial inquiry from the crucial question of whether minorities have equal access to the electoral process to a historical question of individual motives.[16]

The Amendments did not significantly affect the sections of the Act relating to "preclearance" of changes in voting procedures. The Supreme Court has decided a number of cases concerning the preclearance requirements of Section 5 of the Voting Rights Act, with mixed results.

In *City of Rome v. United States*,[17], a Georgia city with no history of voting discrimination was unable to "bail out" of the preclearance system imposed by Section 5 of the Voting Rights Act because the state of Georgia as a whole is subject to Section 5. The Court discussed whether the Section 5 "effects" test may be overinclusive (but it is not clear what weight this discussion has after the 1982 Amendments to Section 2). And in *Hathorn v. Lovorn*,[18] the Supreme Court reasserted federal authority to dictate when

16. S. Rep. No. 97-417 at 16, U.S. Code Cong. & Admin. News, p. 193. The value of the amended Section 2 has been debated extensively. *Compare* Blumstein, *Defining and Proving Race Discrimination: Perspectives on the Purpose vs. Results Approach from the Voting Rights Act*, 69 Va. L. Rev. 633 (1983), *with* Parker, *The "Results" Test of Section 2 of the Voting Rights Act: Abandoning the Intent Standard*, 69 Va. L. Rev. 715 (1983).

The Voting Rights Act Amendments of 1982 also extended the special enforcement provisions of the Act, including the preclearance requirements in Section 5, for an additional 25 years. 42 U.S.C. §1973(c). The Amendments extend the bilingual voter registration and election assistance provisions until 1992. 42 U.S.C. §1973aa-1a.

For content and results of committee hearings, *see* "Extension of the Voting Rights Act: Hearings Before the Subcommittee on Civil and Constitutional Rights of the Committee on the Judiciary," 97th Cong., 1st Sess. 2053 (1981). The extensive Senate and House floor debates on the amendments are summarized in Boyd & Markman, *The 1982 Amendments to the Voting Rights Act: A Legislative History*, 40 Wash. & Lee L. Rev. 1347 (1983), and Note, *Amending Section 2 of the Voting Rights Act of 1965*, 32 Case W. Res. L. Rev. 500 (1982).

The amended Act (P.L. 97-205) was signed by President Ronald Reagan on June 29, 1982. The amended sections can be found at 42 U.S.C.A. §§1973, 1973b, and 1973aa-1a, aa-6 (1983).

For a discussion of the effect of the amendments on the Voting Rights Act, *see* Comment, *The Dilemma of the Voting Rights Act — Recognizing the Emerging Political Equality Norm*, 83 Colum. L. Rev. 1615 (1983); Note, *Eradicating Racial Discrimination in Voter Registration: Rights and Remedies Under the Voting Rights Act Amendments of 1982*, 52 Fordham L. Rev. 93 (1983).

For a discussion of the Voting Rights Act in historical perspective, *see* Note, *Mississippi and the Voting Rights Act, 1965-1982*, 52 Miss. L.J. 803 (1982).

17. 446 U.S. 156 (1980).

18. 457 U.S. 255 (1982). *Compare* City of Port Arthur v. United States, 459 U.S. 159 (1982), which upheld the District of Columbia District Court's refusal to approve changes in a Texas election district until its discriminatory majority vote requirement was changed, *with* City of Lockhart v. United States, 460 U.S. 125 (1983), which overturned invalidation of an electoral system by the same district

Section 5 preclearance requirements apply to state election regulations, holding that the Mississippi Supreme Court erred in approving changes in local election procedures without federal preclearance review.

§4.6.1 Judicial Review and the 1982 Amendments

Courts have found little difficulty in upholding the 1982 Amendments to the Voting Rights Act of 1965, against constitutional challenge. A typical decision is *Major v. Treen.*[19] There, a three judge court overturned a 1981 state law dispersing the black population of Orleans Parish, Louisiana, into two congressional districts, thereby preventing what otherwise would have been a black voting majority in one of the districts. Without much difficulty, the court found that extending the Voting Rights Act's proscription against processes that have a discriminatory impact denying or abridging the right to vote based on race (as opposed to a prohibition limited to intentional discrimination) was within congressional authority to regulate state voting practices pursuant to power granted under the Fifteenth Amendment.

A summary of the long opinion by Judge Politz in *Major v. Treen* illustrates in dramatic fashion why the 1982 Amendments are still needed more than a decade and a half after enactment of the 1965 Voting Rights Act. The suit was a challenge to a 1981 Louisiana statute (Act 20) enacted specifically to prevent a black majority congressional district in New Orleans.

Orleans Parish is now 55 percent black and largely concentrated in one contiguous expanse of the inner city. The need to reapportion after the 1980 census led to a major debate as to whether one district should be made coterminous with the city of New Orleans, an approach that would comply with one-person, one-vote standards, and would not dilute minority votes. The alternative was to divide the black inner city area with mainly white suburban parishes. Blacks urged the former approach. Subsequently, each house of the state legislature prepared a plan that would provide for a mainly black district in New Orleans. But there were those, including the Governor, who opposed the creation of such a district.

---

court, holding that although a new election system did not act to remove effects of past discrimination, it was valid because it did not make things worse for blacks.

See also McDaniel v. Sanchez, 452 U.S. 130 (1981), which upheld the requirement of preclearance for a reapportionment plan for electoral districts in Kleberg County, Texas, an area with a large Hispanic population. For further discussion of preclearance requirements, *see* Motomura, *Preclearance Under Section Five of the Voting Rights Act,* 61 N.C.L. Rev. 189 (1983); Note, *What Constitutes Retrogression Within Section 5 in Ascertaining Discriminatory Effect of Voting Changes,* 23 Washburn L.J. 219 (1983).

19. 574 F. Supp. 325 (E.D. La. 1983).

The legislative process utilized to defeat the mainly black district reads like something out of the nineteenth century, and Judge Politz's opinion reviews it in detail. The Governor objected to a plan that would jeopardize the re-election chances of the incumbent congressman. He also expressed concern about racial polarization which he saw as an inevitable consequence of the deliberate sculpting of districts along racial lines. He characterized it as an attempt by the Louisiana legislature to enact into law the discredited idea of proportional representation along racial lines.

As the court noted, the Governor's concerns were restricted to the aggregation of blacks within one district; the coalescence of whites was not regarded as ominous so long as the incumbent Congressman Livingston's chances for re-election were maximized. "An Orleans-based district with a 55 percent black population was not acceptable to the Governor. . . , an Orleans-based district with a 55 percent white population encountered no objection."[20]

Legislative leaders began meeting secretly in the Senate's computer room, located in the subbasement of the State Capitol, to work out a compromise acceptable to the Governor. The court reported, "black legislators were not invited, those responsible for calling the gathering having decided that the goal of crafting a district with a high minority profile would have to be abandoned."[21]

The whites at the meeting felt the necessity of the Governor's desire to guarantee the re-election of white incumbent Congressman Livingston, and State Representative Boggs. They also wanted a district that was at least 55 percent Jefferson Parish (white). "Hence," the court found, "the participants determined that the minority's interest in obtaining a predominantly black district would have to be sacrificed in order to satisfy both the Governor and the Jefferson Parish group."[22]

As one government official candidly testified, ". . . the feeling in the meeting was that the one group, the one contingency group that was not going to come out of the session satisfied was going to be the blacks. The reason for that was that with all of the competing interests . . . there was probably going to be virtually no way to satisfy the black members of the Legislature . . . insofar as creating a majority black district [was concerned] . . . They [minority legislators] didn't have enough votes."

The conferees finally worked out a scheme that fulfilled their priorities. The boundaries, the court found "are clearly racial in character, selectively segregating white and black residents of New Orleans in the majority white First District and the more heterogeneous Second District."[23] After the

20. 574 F. Supp. at 333.
21. *Id.* at 334.
22. *Id.*
23. *Id.* at 334-335.

Governor approved the plan, a formal conference committee was named. No blacks were appointed.

Over the objections of black leaders, the plan was approved by the committee, adopted by the legislature, and signed by the Governor. The court found a substantial degree of racial polarization exhibited in the voting patterns of Orleans Parish. It also found Louisiana's history of racial discrimination, both de jure and de facto, continues to have an adverse effect on the ability of its black residents to participate fully in the electoral process.

Reviewing the continuing discrimination, the court said, "Such influences, in conjunction with past election practices excluding blacks from the political process, account for the present disparity between black voter registration and black population in Orleans Parish. From the evidence adduced, we are persuaded that they account for the lower black turnout at election time. A sense of futility engendered by the pervasiveness of prior discrimination, both public and private, is perceived as discouraging blacks from entering into the governmental process."

The court found that Section 2 of the 1982 Amendments "dispenses with the requirement that a plaintiff demonstrate intentional discrimination in the imposition or maintenance of the disputed electoral structure." And reviewing Congressional power under the Constitution to protect voting rights against discrimination, the court rejected state claims that §2 exceeded Congressional power and usurped the judiciary's exclusive prerogative to define the limits of the Constitution.[24]

The court, having found plaintiffs made out a prima facie case of voter dilution in violation of §2, noted that while "several black candidates, among them Mayor Morial, have won office in Orleans Parish [that fact] does not foreclose a finding of dilution. . . . Considering the parish's 55 percent black population, the 15 percent success rate of black candidates at the polls is substantially lower than might be anticipated absent such impediments to black voting and registration as the lingering ramifications of historic disenfranchisement conjoined with past and present disparities in education, income, employment and housing."[25]

"If Act 20's sundering of the black population of New Orleans were allowed to stand, the effective independent impact of black voters would be unfairly and illegally minimized." The court said, "we are not unmindful of the legitimate debate among academics and courts about the relative merits of concentrating a minority population within one district or dividing that population into two or more districts so that it exerts a substantial influence in each. We are convinced that in the present case, the division of

24. *Id.* at 341-343.
25. *Id.* at 351.

the black population was not designed to enhance the effectiveness of the black electorate, nor is it likely to occasion such."[26]

§4.11.1 *The At-Large District: A By-Gone Proposition?*

Even without the evidentiary benefits civil rights plaintiffs are likely to gain from the 1982 Amendments to the Voting Rights Act, there have been an increasing number of successful challenges to at-large local election districts in recent years. One line of cases has acknowledged the necessity of showing a discriminatory purpose in the use of at-large systems, and courts in these cases have accepted convincing indirect evidence to establish discrimination. This was the tack taken in *Mobile v. Bolden* on remand.[27]

The result in *Perkins v. City of West Helena*[28] is typical when the facts are strongly indicative of discriminatory purpose. The city has a 40 percent black and 60 percent white population. Since 1920, it has elected a council of eight aldermen (two each from four wards, two all-white and two racially mixed). Candidates must specify post or seat, and then run at-large with each voter having two votes for each ward. No blacks have been elected and the elected white officials were unresponsive to minority interests. The court reviewed the law, and concluded that even after *Bolden*, it protects more than the simple right to vote, particularly given the city's unsavory record of efforts to prevent blacks from voting.[29]

The Supreme Court adopted this approach with *Rogers v. Lodge*.[30] The Court declared Burke County, Georgia's at-large election system

26. *Id.* at 352-354. Judge Politz's rationale and finding of constitutionality of Section 2 in Major v. Treen, was adopted by the Fifth Circuit in Jones v. City of Lubbock, 727 F.2d 364, 375 n.6 (5th Cir. 1984). In this case, the appeals court found that proof of purposeful discrimination in the city's adherence to the at-large system of electing its city council was inadequate to constitute a violation of the Fifteenth Amendment, but that the evidence did make out a violation of Section 2.

27. 542 F. Supp. 1050 (S.D. Ala. 1982). *See also* Broussard v. Perez, 686 F.2d 320 (5th Cir. 1982)(used *Zimmer* factors to find intent to deprive blacks of equal protection in maintenance of an at-large method of electing members of parish commission); Perkins v. City of West Helena, 675 F.2d 201 (8th Cir. 1982), *aff'd without opinion*, 459 U.S. 801 (1982)(at-large system of electing aldermen was unconstitutionally maintained to limit chances of blacks participating meaningfully in the political process and electing legislators of their choice).

28. 675 F.2d 201 (8th Cir. 1982), *aff'd without opinion*, 459 U.S. 801 (1982).

29. *See also*, Political Civil Voters Org. v. City of Terrell, 565 F. Supp 338 (N.D. Tex. 1983)(citing history of severe segregation and interference with black voting).

30. 458 U.S. 613 (1982), *aff'g*, Lodge v. Buxton, 639 F.2d 1358 (5th Cir. 1981). The case is noted at 96 Harv. L. Rev. 106 (1982). The editors found that while the opinion gave lip service to the *City of Mobile* holding that at-large districts are not per se unconstitutional, they concluded, "*Rogers* seems inconsistent with much of the language and analysis of the plurality in *Mobile*."

invalid, finding that although the system had no discriminatory purpose when it was enacted in 1911, the electoral structure was maintained after 1965 for discriminatory reasons. Intent was inferred from the fact that no blacks had ever been elected to the county commission, officials were unresponsive to minority interests, and segregation and discrimination were rife in other areas of public conduct (education, housing, civil service employment). Justice White, speaking for the majority in the 6-3 decision, also noted the "depressed socio-economic status" of blacks in Burke County.

Some courts welcomed the Supreme Court's return to pre-*Mobile* proof standards. In affirming a lower court's application of the *Zimmer* standards to invalidate at-large elections for county commissioners, the Fifth Circuit confessed that "the *Bolden* Court's divergent analysis on the intentional discrimination issue left us somewhat 'adrift on uncharted seas with respect to how to proceed.' "[31] The cases that have upheld at-large election districts have found that neither discriminatory purpose nor effect was proven.[32]

In the wake of the 1982 Voting Rights Act Amendments, several courts have eschewed requiring any showing of intentional discrimination when an at-large system acts to dilute black voting power.[33] In *Jordan v. City of Greenwood*,[34] the Fifth Circuit remanded a challenge to an at-large system for reconsideration in light of the 1982 Amendments.

§4.15.3 Redistricting Challenges: The Racial Cases

The shocking facts in *Gomillion v. Lightfoot*,[35] revealing the determination of a state legislature to deny blacks the vote by redrawing a town's boundaries so as to exclude virtually all black voters, made clear to the Supreme Court that it could not in good conscience continue adherence to its traditional refusal to enter what it called the "political thicket" of reap-

31. McMillan v. Escambia Co. Fla., 688 F.2d 960 (1982).

32. Leadership Roundtable v. City of Little Rock, 661 F.2d 701 (8th Cir. 1981)(plaintiffs did not show sufficient dilution of black vote); United States v. Dallas County Commission, 548 F. Supp. 794, 875 (S.D. Ala. 1982)(court held that despite past discrimination black voters now are able to participate fully in elections).

For more discussion of the future of at-large elections, see, Crosby, *At-Large Congressional Elections: A By-Gone Proposition*, 38 J. Mo. B. 266 (1982); O'Rourke, *Constitutional and Statutory Challenges to Local At-Large Elections*, 17 U. Rich. L. Rev. 39 (1982). See also, Comment, *Constitutional Significance of the Discriminatory Effects of At-Large Elections*, 91 Yale L.J. 974 (1982).

33. *See, e.g.,* Buchanan v. City of Jackson, 708 F.2d 1066 (6th Cir. 1983), which reversed dismissal of a challenge to at-large election, allowing plaintiffs to amend the complaint to reflect the 1982 Amendments. The court found that intentional discrimination was an alternate ground for hearing the case.

34. 711 F.2d 667 (5th Cir. 1983).

35. 364 U.S. 339 (1960). See discussion in the Second Edition, §4.8.

portionment issues. *Gomillion* then paved the way for the Court to develop the "one person, one vote" standard for evaluating the constitutional fairness of reapportionment schemes.[36]

The racial cases, though, have developed along a different and more exacting line of proof than those alleging mathematical inequality in the apportionment process. In the latter, proof of representational disparity between districts of similar size sufficed to entitle relief, but in racial cases, plaintiffs' allegations of gerrymandered districts or adherence to at-large voting must be supported by proof that such policies were intended to have a racially discriminatory effect.

One can assume that the heightened proof requirements after *City of Mobile* have been returned to normal by Section 2 of the 1982 Amendments to the Voting Rights Act. Moreover, the language of the new Section 2 is likely to encourage legislatures to draft and courts to approve "safe districts," defined by the Justice Department as districts in which blacks "have a reasonable chance of electing a candidate of their choice."[37] It is less clear what impact will occur on racial issues as a result of more recent reapportionment decisions that seem to be abandoning the relative neutrality of mathematical equality — a standard that permitted the most flagrant forms of political gerrymandering — in favor of a more difficult to define, but potentially more fair, "good faith" standard.

In 1983 the Supreme Court decided a pair of reapportionment cases that seem explainable on this new "good faith" approach. First, a 5-4 majority overturned the 1980 New Jersey state legislative reapportionment scheme in *Karcher v. Daggett*,[38] even though the maximum population deviation between districts was less than one percent. The Court held that the state had not shown a good faith effort to achieve equality. The state contended that the districts were drawn so as to preserve the voting strength of minority groups, but the Court held that no relationship had been shown between the district lines chosen and minority voting power.

The New Jersey plan resulted in a bizarre configuration of districts with little contiguity or relation to county lines (a number of municipal areas were preserved as single districts). The majority opinion did not address this evident gerrymandering, but Justice Stevens suggested it as an alternate ground for the decision in his concurrence. Stevens, and the dissent, would not uphold a redistricting plan where gerrymandering was present, even if perfect numerical equality had been achieved. Justice Stevens suggested that the district lines were drawn to preserve Democratic Party strength in the state.[39]

36. *See, e.g.*, Reynolds v. Sims, 377 U.S. 533 (1964).

37. Howard and Howard, *The Dilemma of the Voting Rights Act—Recognizing the Emerging Political Equality Norm*, 83 Colum. L. Rev. 1615, n.3 (1983).

38. 103 S. Ct. 2653 (1983).

39. *Karcher* is noted at 97 Harv. L. Rev. 135 (1983).

A companion case, *Brown v. Thompson*,[40] upheld Wyoming's recent reapportionment of state representatives, despite an average population deviation of 15 percent and a maximum deviation of 89 percent. This result was justified by Wyoming's long-standing and nondiscriminatory policy of allocating at least one representative to each county. Also, the entire system was not challenged, but only the allocation of one representative to Wyoming's smallest county, which by itself did not cause such a large deviation between districts. Reading *Karcher* and *Brown* together strengthens the impression that the Supreme Court is no longer relying heavily on numerical indicia of disproportionate representation, but has adopted a more politically sensitive "good faith" standard to measure constitutional violations.

In racial cases, similar "good faith" results require the statutory authority of the Voting Rights Act of 1965, as amended, or a strong showing of intentional discrimination using *Zimmer*-type evidentiary measuring rods. These standards are sufficient in blatant cases like the New Orleans reapportionment disgrace struck down in *Major v. Treen*.[41] In future cases, the proof of discriminatory intent may be less clear, and the claims of other groups to "political equality" more urgent. At that point, history suggests, and may even require, a prediction that the gravitational pull on these issues will favor the subordination of black voter claims.

It is at that point that the plea of black activist Faith Ann Courage[42] for proportional racial representation — a plea now specifically barred by Section 2 of the 1982 Amendments[43] — will again become a perhaps unfortunate choice, but the only practical means of providing the affirmative relief blacks need to gain political parity in a nation committed still to the concept accepted by white Republicans and Democrats alike in the 1870's: "Blacks should vote, but should not hold office."[44]

40. 103 S. Ct. 2690 (1983).

41. In *Rybicki v. State Board of Elections of Illinois*, 574 F. Supp. 1082 (N.D. Ill. 1982), the 1981 state redistricting plan was held to unconstitutionally dilute black voting strength. The court ruled that limited consideration of partisan advantage did not invalidate the plan, and that the plan did not disadvantage Hispanic voters.

42. See Second Edition, §4.18 Racism Hypo: Delta County Black Voters v. Delta County.

43. "*Provided*, That nothing in this section establishes a right to have members of a protected class elected in numbers equal to their proportion in the population." 42 U.S.C. §1973(f)(2) (1982).

44. Bolden v. City of Mobile, 542 F. Supp. 1050, 1059 (S.D. Ala. 1982).

Chapter 5
Discrimination in the Administration of Justice

§5.5.1 18 U.S.C. §§241 and 242

There have been few new developments in the interpretation of the criminal statutes covering violations of civil rights, 18 U.S.C. §§241 and 242. These statutes continue to be useful, though inadequate components of the civil rights arsenal. As always, their efficacy depends on the commitment of the authorities who have the power to use them, a factor that varies both with individual administrators and with successive political regimes.

One new area of civil rights protection affecting racial minorities is the rights of persons entering the United States illegally. In a case of first impression, the Ninth Circuit held that illegal aliens are included in the language of §242 protecting any inhabitant of any "State, Territory or District."[1] The decision upheld the §242 convictions of federal Border Patrol agents in California who routinely beat Mexican aliens while transporting them to processing centers. The court gave no credence to the defendants' argument that though the statute itself covers deprivations of rights on account of such inhabitant being an alien, the language refers only to legal aliens. The court found a clear legislative intent to include all persons within the boundaries of the United States as inhabitants, without reference to their legal status.[2] However, aliens — legal or illegal — are not covered by the companion statute, §241, which protects only "citizens."

1. United States v. Otherson, 637 F.2d 1276 (9th Cir. 1980), *cert. denied*, 454 U.S. 840 (1981).
2. 637 F.2d at 1285.

§5.6 Civil Remedies Under 42 U.S.C. §1983: Update

After many years of restrictive interpretation, the decision in *Monell v. New York City Dept. of Social Services*[3] that municipalities and other local governmental units were not immune from §1983 liability, opened up significant applications for 42 U.S.C. §1983. The past five years have seen a flood of §1983 suits, and several attempts by the Supreme Court to define the boundaries of the statute.

This task is made more difficult because many of the suits initiated under §1983 in recent years have had little to do with the traditional civil rights issues of race, sex, religion, or ethnicity. Some involve injuries usually classified as simple torts, such as negligent loss of property.[4] An increasing number of §1983 suits are filed on behalf of corporations.[5] Such inappropriate or frivolous use of the statute clogs the courts, irritates judges, and diverts attention from worthier civil rights cases. While race has not been a central issue in the major post-*Monell* decisions, these cases show the Court's concern with preserving §1983 as a tool against serious civil rights abuses while discouraging inappropriate suits.

In *Owen v. City of Independence*,[6] the Supreme Court confirmed the language in *Monell* indicating that municipalities, as well as other local governmental units are "persons" within the scope of §1983. The case involved a police chief who was summarily fired when city officials learned that an investigation had uncovered evidence of misconduct in the police department. The Supreme Court held that the city was not immune from §1983 liability, and that it could not assert the good faith of city officials as a defense.[7]

The Court interpreted other language in §1983 liberally in *Maine v. Thiboutot*,[8] finding that the phrase "rights, privileges, or immunities secured by the Constitution and laws" encompasses claims based purely on federal statutory law. The appellate court had argued that the words "and laws" had been included in the statute inadvertently and that only §1983 claims with Constitutional dimensions should be heard. The Supreme Court refused to accept this interpretation of legislative history and held that the Thiboutots, a family deprived of welfare benefits, could state a §1983 claim based on the Social Security Act without asserting a constitutional claim.[9] Justice Powell dissented, warning that if any federal statute could be the basis for a civil rights claim, the courts would soon be deluged by claims

3. Monell v. New York City Dept. of Social Services, 436 U.S. 658 (1978).
4. Parratt v. Taylor, 451 U.S. 527 (1981).
5. Newport v. Facts Concerts, Inc., 453 U.S. 247 (1981).
6. Owen v. City of Independence, 445 U.S. 622 (1980).
7. *Id.* at 638.
8. Maine v. Thiboutot, 448 U.S. 1 (1980).
9. *Id.* at 4.

based on statutes controlling anadromous fisheries and historic preservation.[10]

But in some respects, the Court has been equally concerned about establishing limits to §1983 liability. *Parratt v. Taylor*[11] established that negligent actions, even those resulting in a deprivation of civil rights, are not sufficient basis for a §1983 claim. In that case an inmate whose mail-order hobby kit had been lost by prison officials was told that his claim should have been pursued through the Nebraska tort claims procedure. The decision stressed that though this particular case involved property, rather than personal, rights, and though the property was worth only a trivial amount ($23.50), the basis for dismissal was the negligent manner of the injury, not its magnitude.[12]

In *Newport v. Facts Concerts, Inc.*[13] the Court overturned an award of punitive damages against a municipality while upholding the compensatory portion of the judgement. The plaintiff in this case was the corporation responsible for organizing the Newport Jazz Festival. Its complaint was that city officials attempted to cancel its contract over a dispute about whether one of the acts booked was a jazz or a rock group and that the resultant publicity had caused ticket sales to slump. The city had acted without investigating whether its characterization of the objectionable act was correct and against the advice of its legal counsel. The Court found that though municipalities were not immune from liability at the time §1983 was enacted, they were immune to punitive damage awards.[14] The rationale was that though local government bodies should be made to compensate those whose rights have been injured, punishment would unfairly affect the citizens and taxpayers of the city.[15] However, in a recent decision, *Smith v. Wade*, the Supreme Court held that where the official conduct was the result of a reckless or callous disregard of the rights or safety of others, punitive damages were appropriate.[16] In that case, a prison inmate was placed in a cell with two other inmates who harassed and sexually assaulted him.

Judicial response to the increased importance of §1983 varies widely. Some courts have been quick to accept the expansion of local governmental liability as a useful civil rights tool, while others are concerned primarily with the increased burden any recognition of a right places upon the court system. The Supreme Court has been subject to both of these influences, but has so far kept to the middle ground, seeking to limit the use of §1983 where inappropriate while preserving its availability to redress serious civil rights violations. However, the Court has not formulated this aim in a way

10. *Id.* at 23, Powell, J., dissenting.
11. Parratt v. Taylor, 451 U.S. 527 (1981).
12. *Id.* at 543.
13. Newport v. Facts Concerts, Inc., 453 U.S. 247 (1981).
14. *Id.* at 259.
15. *Id.* at 263.
16. Smith v. Wade, 461 U.S. 30 (1983).

that focuses on traditionally disadvantaged groups. There is a danger that if the flood of civil rights claims in which unconventional plaintiffs outnumber minorities continues to overload the courts, at some point the Supreme Court will change its emphasis and limit the scope of §1983 more substantively.

Presently, at least, the Supreme Court is resisting attempts to limit the application of §1983 through abolishment of long-standing civil rights precedents. In *Patsy v. Florida Board of Regents*,[17] the Fifth Circuit dismissed the §1983 claim of a woman alleging racial and sexual discrimination by Florida International University. The court acknowledged that the rule against requiring exhaustion of administrative remedies was firmly established, but contended that the time had come to reevaluate the rule. The Supreme Court accepted this challenge and reversed, strongly supporting the no exhaustion rule, and citing a long line of precedents, beginning with *McNeese v. Board of Education*, for the Fifth Circuit's benefit.[18] Though this decision was comforting to civil rights supporters, it remains discouraging that even a rule backed by a generation of precedents should be subject to periodic challenge.

§5.7.1 The Civil Rights Attorney's Fees Awards Act of 1976

The Supreme Court's 1975 decision in *Alyeska Pipeline Service Co. v. Wilderness Society*[19] upset a lower court's award of attorney fees by ruling that such awards required specific congressional authorization. In the aftermath of *Alyeska*, Congress enacted the Civil Rights Attorney's Fees Awards Act of 1976,[20] which allows discretionary awards of reasonable attorney fees to the prevailing party in suits brought under §§1981, 1982, 1983, 1985, Title VI, and Title IX. This statute may be at least partially responsible for the "explosion in civil rights cases"[21] in the late 1970's and early 1980's. Though it merely authorized the established practice of many lower federal courts in civil rights cases,[22] the Act may well encourage more attorneys and clients to pursue their claims. It certainly will not discourage them. However, since a party must prevail to claim fees under the Act, and because long years of work generally precede any decision in a civil rights case, the eventual availability of attorney fees is not likely to be the sole motivation for filing suit.

17. Patsy v. Florida Board of Regents, 634 F.2d 900 (5th Cir. 1981).

18. Patsy v. Florida Board of Regents, 457 U.S. 496, 500 (1982) (citing McNeese v. Board of Education, 373 U.S. 668 (1963)).

19. 421 U.S. 240 (1975).

20. Act of Oct. 19, 1976, 90 Stat. 2641, *codified at* 41 U.S.C.A. §1988 (1983).

21. *The Firestorm Over Attorney Fee Awards*, 69 A.B.A.J. 1420 (1983).

22. *Id.*

The Supreme Court's first analysis of the factors to be used in determining reasonable fees under §1988 was *Hensley v. Eckerhart*,[23] decided in the 1982 term. In a 5-4 decision the Court held that a plaintiff may be awarded fees only for legal work performed on prevailing claims. Then in *Blum v. Stenson*,[24] the Court addressed the measure of fees to be awarded, particularly to nonprofit legal organizations. In a Medicaid suit brought by the New York Legal Aid Society, the Court, approving an award of $90 to $100 per hour, read the reasonable fee provision of the federal statute to mean fees generally paid in the area for legal work of a similar character, rather than the actual cost of the work performed. On the other hand, the Court found the record did not support the trial court's grant of a 50 percent bonus because of the uniqueness of the case, the difficulty of the work, and the risk involved in bringing the matter to court.

The *Blum* decision may bring needed stability to attorney fee issues, and prevent situations in which, for example, a New York City case decided the same year as *Blum*, awarded a Wall Street firm only $60 an hour.[25] But *Blum's* principal value is in making clear that a nonprofit legal organization or a private firm doing pro bono work should not be limited to fees on a cost basis rather than the "market rate" simply because it would have handled the case even if fees weren't available.

Though the willingness of the firm to take on a case without compensation should not be decisive, a noninflationary fee standard is highly advisable for both profit and nonprofit firms. This is especially true because a large proportion of the defendants in actions covered by §1988 are public officials and local governments whose expenses will in the end be paid by the public. Given this fact, awards made large through emphasis on the punitive aspects of attorney fees could jeopardize §1988.

§5.15.3 The Peremptory Challenge: The Swain *Barrier Persists*

Despite increasing criticism,[26] the systematic exclusion standard of *Swain v. Alabama*[27] remains the rule applied when minorities charge that peremptory challenges are being used by prosecutors to exclude them from petit juries. Almost 20 years after the decision, virtually no convictions have been reversed on the basis of *Swain*. The exceptions, a series of cases

23. 461 U.S. 424.
24. 104 S. Ct. 1541 (1984).
25. McCann v. Coughlin, 698 F.2d 112 (2d Cir. 1983).
26. *See, e.g.*, McCray v. New York, 103 S. Ct. 2438, 2440-2443 (1983)(Marshall, J., dissenting from denial of certiorari. Justice Marshall argues that the *Swain* decision should be reconsidered).
27. Swain v. Alabama, 380 U.S. 202 (1965).

from Louisiana's East Baton Rouge Parish, prove that it is impractical, and often impossible, to establish the case after case exclusion of blacks required by the systematic exclusion standard.

In *State v. Brown*[28] the Louisiana Supreme Court held that a record of 14 cases alleging illegal use of peremptory challenges in the same parish within eight years established a pattern of systematic exclusion that met the requirements of *Swain.* The same year another conviction from the same parish was reversed, relying on the record in *Brown.*[29] In both of these cases the prosecutor had admitted in an investigatory hearing that he routinely challenged blacks without inquiring into their attitudes or prejudices.[30] But less than three years later a conviction in the same parish, with the same prosecutor, was upheld because the defendant had not put into evidence the information that had established a pattern of exclusion of blacks in the earlier cases.[31] In this case, though the prosecutor had used 14 of his 18 peremptory challenges to exclude blacks, one black actually served on the jury. The court cited this as evidence that the record of exclusion in the past should not be routinely accepted as proof of exclusion in the present.[32]

The use of peremptory challenges to rid juries of blacks in racially sensitive cases is not a justice-denying policy limited to the South. In dissenting from the refusal to grant review in three capital cases from Illinois involving black defendants, Justice Marshall, joined by Justice Brennan, noted that "[w]henever a Negro defendant is charged with a capital offense, there is a substantial chance that the prosecution will employ its peremptory challenges to remove Negroes and other minorities from the jury panel.[33]

Supporting his concern with statistics, Marshall reported that in petitioner Hernando Williams's case, 22 percent of the venire was black, the prosecution used 11 of its 20 peremptory challenges to exclude blacks, and an all-white jury sentenced Williams to death.[34] In the case of Wendell Dixon, 20 percent of the venire was black, and the prosecution used five of seven peremptory challenges to exclude all black members from the venire. An all-white jury then convicted Dixon and sentenced him to death. Finally, in the case of Lonnie Yates, the record is silent as to the percentage of blacks on the venire, but the State used 13 of 16 peremptory challenges to remove blacks from the venire. The jury that convicted Yates and sentenced him to death included a single black person.

28. State v. Brown, 371 So. 2d 751 (La. 1979).
29. State v. Washington, 375 So. 2d 1162 (La. 1979).
30. *Id.* at 1163.
31. State v. Hayes, 414 So. 2d 717 (La. 1982).
32. *Id.* at 720.
33. Williams v. Illinois, 104 S. Ct. 2364, 2365 (1984) (dissenting from denial of certiorari).
34. *Id.* Petitioner Williams pled guilty, and the jury heard only the sentencing phase of his trial.

Since 1959, Marshall said, the Supreme Court of Illinois has reviewed at least 33 cases in which criminal defendants have alleged prosecutorial misuse of peremptory challenges to exclude black jurors. And since the enactment of the latest Illinois Death Act, 29 juries have been empanelled to sentence black defendants in capital cases. Nineteen of these juries were all white, and five had only one black juror. Marshall found it "simply inconceivable that the racial composition of these juries was the result of statistical anomaly."[35]

§5.16.1 The Wheeler/Soares *Alternative*

Though the alternatives to the *Swain* rule created in *People v. Wheeler*[36] and *Commonwealth v. Soares*[37] have engendered much discussion, neither state nor federal courts outside of California and Massachusetts seem eager to follow them. Several states have voiced criticism of the rule in *Swain*, noting particularly that it is a standard that allows no practical relief for minorities that are the victims of exclusion by peremptory challenge.[38] But these states are also concerned with preserving the peremptory challenge as a useful tool, and are very suspicious of any rule that would require attorneys to explain or limit their use of peremptory challenges.

Much of the reluctance to follow the *Wheeler/Soares* alternatives stems from the weaknesses of those standards. The most common objection is that the separation of peremptory challenges into those for "specific" and those for "group" bias destroys the attorney's discretion to use peremptory challenges, and that the categorization itself is not rational.[39] Many states find the standard imprecise and difficult to apply, and refrain for that rea-

35. *Id.* Citing the most recent census figures, Marshall said that 14.56 percent of Illinois population is black, and thus if the jury-selection process in Illinois was completely race-blind, roughly 17 percent of all juries would be expected to have one or no black jurors. "In fact," Marshall reported, "more than 80 percent of the Illinois sentencing juries have had less than two Negro members when the defendant is a Negro." *Id.* at 2366.

36. 22 Cal. 3d 258, 583 P.2d 748 (1978).

37. 377 Mass. 461, 387 N.E.2d 499 (1979), *cert. denied*, 444 U.S. 881 (1980). The *Soares* approach was recently extended to grand jury selection by the Massachusetts Supreme Judicial Court in Commonwealth v. Aponte, — Mass. — (1984).

38. *See, e.g.*, State v. Crespin, 612 P.2d 716 (N. Mex. App. 1980); Johnson v. State, 418 So. 2d 1063 (Fla. App. 1982); Saunders v. State, 401 A.2d 629 (Del. 1979). *But cf.* Commonwealth v. Henderson, 438 A.2d 951 (Penn. 1981); State v. Eames, 365 So. 2d 1361 (La. 1978) (supporting *Swain* standard).

39. Fredric P. Andes, *Discriminatory Use of Peremptory Challenges and the Protection of Defendant and Group Rights*, written work requirement, Harvard Law School, 1980.

son.[40] Some states have no constitutional language analogous to that used in *Wheeler* and *Soares*, or are uncomfortable with diverging from federal constitutional law in the civil rights area.[41] And, of course, standards based on state constitutions are of no help in federal courts, where a large proportion of civil rights cases are heard.

A few states have considered *Wheeler/Soares* seriously. Appellate courts in both Illinois and New York have followed *Wheeler*. The decisions in Illinois are in conflict with another division of that state's appellate court; the New York Court of Appeals has recently rejected the *Wheeler/Soares* approach.[42] Courts in several states appear willing to follow the California and Massachusetts approach but have not found an appropriate case with which to do so.[43] Though the area remains generally unsatisfactory to both state and federal courts, there does not seem to be any great momentum developing to jump on the *Wheeler/Soares* bandwagon.

§5.17.1 Raising the Racial Issue on Voir Dire: Recent Cases

While at present minority jurors may be peremptorily excluded from juries without much recourse, minority defendants are not so easily given the opportunity to identify and challenge jurors who have racial prejudices. In *Rosales-Lopez v. United States*[44] the Supreme Court followed the trend set in *Ristaino v. Ross*,[45] holding that the right to question prospective jurors as to racial prejudice in voir dire is constitutionally protected only when racial issues are inextricably bound up in the trial. The Court held that federal courts should follow a somewhat stricter standard, allowing racial questioning when the defendant requests it, the defendant is accused of a violent crime, and the defendant and victim are of different races. The defendant in *Rosales-Lopez*, who was a Mexican-American accused of smuggling illegal aliens into the United States, requested voir dire questions regarding the

40. *See, e.g.,* State v. Sims, 639 S.W.2d 105 (Mo. App. 1982); State v. Raymond, 446 A.2d 743 (R.I. 1982); People v. Smith, 622 P.2d 90 (Colo. App. 1980).

41. Patri v. Percy, 530 F. Supp. 591 (E.D. Wis. 1982).

42. Illinois: People v. Payne, 436 N.E.2d 1046 (Ill. App. Ct. 1982)(third division followed *Wheeler*); People v. Teague, 439 N.E.2d 1066 (Ill. App. Ct. 1982)(first division noted *Payne* and followed *Swain*). New York: People v. Thompson, 435 N.Y.S.2d 739 (N.Y. App. Div. 1981)(followed *Wheeler*); People v. McCray, 457 N.Y.S.2d 441 (N.Y. 1982), *cert. denied* 103 S. Ct. 2438 (1983) (rejected *Wheeler* and *Soares*).

43. *See, e.g.,* State v. Crespin, 612 P.2d 717 (N. Mex. App. 1980); Mallott v. State, 608 P.2d 737 (Alaska 1980).

44. Rosales-Lopez v. United States, 451 U.S. 182 (1981).

45. Ristaino v. Ross, 424 U.S. 589 (1976).

jurors' attitudes toward Mexican-Americans and aliens. The Court held that since the crime was not violent, and the defendant was a member of the same minority as the victims, no racial issue was raised.[46]

The federal courts' reluctance to discover racial issues and the difficulty of meeting the federal standard to require racial questioning are illustrated in *United States v. Dickens.*[47] In that case *Rosales-Lopez* was cited to support the holding that specific questions as to racial or religious prejudices were permissible but not required where the defendants did not specifically request them. The defendants were members of a black Muslim separatist group charged with racketeering and armed robbery to raise money for their religious organization. The court asked only general questions regarding the jurors' impartiality.[48]

At least one state court has shown an inclination to recognize racial issues, at least when prompted. In recent years the Massachusetts courts have identified several sets of circumstances where, as a matter of law, racial issues are presumed to be present. In *Commonwealth v. Stephens*[49] this set of circumstances was expanded to include the situation in which a black man was charged with deriving support from the efforts of a white prostitute, where the evidence would include allegations of violent behavior. Other cases where a racial issue is presumed are those involving interracial rape or sexual offenses against children. The distinction from the federal standard is not in strictness, for the Massachusetts standard, as enunciated, seems at least as strict as the federal. It is the willingness to use the standard to discover racial issues that is refreshing.

46. 451 U.S. at 192.

47. United States v. Dickens, 695 F.2d 765 (3d Cir. 1982), *cert. denied,* 103 S. Ct. 1792 (1983).

48. 695 F.2d at 774.

49. Commonwealth v. Stephens, 15 Mass. App. Ct. 461, 446 N.E.2d 410 (1983).

Chapter 6
Potentials of Protest, Parameters of Protection

§6.2 *The Lawful Protester's Dilemma*

In mid-1984, the question for the civil rights strategist is not only what method of protest will be effective and still gain First Amendment protection, but what subjects of discrimination will lend themselves to protest activity during a period when economic disadvantage that is not easily linked to overt racial bias is the overwhelming barrier to upward movement for blacks.

Large public issues, including abortion, nuclear plants and weapons, and equal rights for women and gays, all have been the subjects of marches, picketing, and rallies. Blacks have not abandoned these techniques to protest continuing discrimination, and have continued to risk arrest with sit-ins in public places to dramatize deeply felt concerns, but these have been tactics adopted for local problems that seldom come to national attention.

As reviewed in Chapter 4, blacks have given more emphasis to the political potential in voting. The success of organized voting efforts resulting in a black mayor in Chicago and almost resulting in a black governor of California, have stimulated the commitment of further energy in this area.

§6.10.1 *The Port Gibson Boycott Litigation Resolved*

More than 15 years after the initiation of the Port Gibson boycott, the suit by white merchants seeking to end that very successful effort, and to cripple, if not destroy, the NAACP, was resolved by the United States Supreme Court in *NAACP v. Claiborne Hardware Co.*[1] In an unanimous decision (Justice Marshall abstaining) the Court vacated a permanent injunction against the boycott and overturned a massive state court judgment

1. 458 U.S. 886 (1982).

awarded against the NAACP and individual boycott participants. Justice Powell's strong opinion emphasized that nonviolent political boycotts are protected under the First Amendment and that organizers of such boycotts may not be held liable for individual acts of violence without proof that they condoned such illegal acts and that the damages were proximately caused by the violence.

Although it received less law review comment than the Eighth Circuit's affirmance of *Missouri v. National Organization for Women*,[2] the *Claiborne* decision is the more significant. The *NOW* case held, not for the first time, that political boycotts are not within the ambit of the Sherman Antitrust Act. The *Claiborne* decision addresses and thwarts most of the devices that have been used by state courts to halt political boycotts and to penalize participants.

The trial court in *Claiborne* granted a permanent injunction against the Port Gibson boycott and a judgment of more than $1,250,000 against the NAACP and 129 individual defendants on three theories. First, the trial court found that the boycott participants had conspired to commit the tort of malicious interference with business. Second, the boycott was held to violate a Mississippi statute prohibiting secondary boycotts that was enacted two years after the Port Gibson boycott began. Third, the boycott was held to violate a Mississippi antitrust statute because it diverted patronage from white merchants to black. Because the second and third theories prohibited even nonviolent boycotts, the trial court neither made extensive fact findings linking the defendants with the several incidents of violence and coercion that had occurred, nor required proof that defendants had conspired to use violence or coercion to enforce the boycott. The judgment represented the entire loss in business to plaintiff merchants over the seven years of the boycott, plus generous attorney fees, costs, and interest.

On appeal, the Mississippi Supreme Court ruled that the statute prohibiting secondary boycotts did not apply to boycotts commenced before its enactment and that the Mississippi antitrust act, like the Sherman Act, did not apply to political boycotts. However, the court affirmed the injunction and the damages award on the common law theory of malicious interference with business, though it did question the methods used to calculate damages. Without remanding for further fact finding, the court found that "many" black citizens were "intimidated" by "threats" of "social ostracism, vilification, and traduction" and that the entire boycott was tainted by this use of force.[3] The court held that liability could be imposed on defendants who acted as "store watchers" or otherwise participated in the boycott, or merely attended meetings of the Claiborne County branch of the NAACP,

2. 467 F. Supp. 289 (W.D. Mo. 1979), *aff'd*, 620 F.2d 1301 (8th Cir), *cert. denied*, 449 U.S. 842 (1980).

3. NAACP v. Claiborne Hardware, Inc., 393 So. 2d 1290, 1299 (Miss. 1980).

and against the national NAACP because it had not "repudiated" the boycott. Thirty-eight defendants were dismissed for lack of proof, leaving 92 defendants jointly and severally liable.[4] The effect of this decision was to impose draconian penalties against all organizers and participants in a political boycott for any isolated incident of violence or coercion, thus effectively chilling the use of boycotts in Mississippi.

The Supreme Court's opinion by Justice Stevens refused to accept the Mississippi Supreme Court's ambiguous findings, emphasizing that the record showed that incidents of violence were few and limited to the early years of the boycott, that the victims of such incidents had continued patronizing white merchants, and that the success of the boycott was due to widespread support in the black community.

Though any defendants who used force could be held liable for damages proximately caused by that force, the Supreme Court held that they would not be liable for the consequences of their nonviolent, protected activity. Civil liability may not be imposed merely because an individual belongs to a group, some members of which commit acts of violence, without proof that the group itself possesses unlawful goals. Likewise, liability cannot be imposed on an organization such as the NAACP because its agents organized a political boycott, or even participated in unauthorized acts of violence. The case was remanded to determine the liability of the few defendants who allegedly participated in violent or coercive incidents.

The *Claiborne* decision makes it virtually impossible for a state or local court to discourage boycotts by imposing tort liability for lost business on participants. Though it is a striking victory for the NAACP, freed from the threat of a massive judgment after all these years; for the majority of the individual defendants whose cases were dismissed; and for all those who would use boycotts as a tool for change, the victory came at great cost. The NAACP was forced to spend massive amounts of time and money to defend this case. While attorney fees and legal costs may be recovered, initially the NAACP had to absorb the entire cost of its defense (and of the many defendants represented by NAACP counsel). In the meantime, the Port Gibson boycott, though effective, was not allowed to accomplish its goals, and many other substantive causes have been neglected during the long years of organization-threatening litigation.

§6.12.1 Boycotts and the NOW Case

The Eighth Circuit's decision in *Missouri v. National Organization for Women, Inc.*,[5] is perhaps the most discussed political boycott case in recent

4. *Id.* at 1302.

5. 620 F.2d 1301 (8th Cir.), *cert. denied*, 449 U.S. 842 (1980), *aff'g* 467 F. Supp. 289 (W.D. Mo. 1979).

years.[6] Holding that the Sherman Antitrust Act is not applicable to political boycotts, such as the NOW's policy of withholding convention business from states that had not ratified the Equal Rights Amendment, the court of appeals approved the district court's refusal to enjoin the NOW boycott. Though not precisely analogous to most racial boycott situations, this decision, taken together with the result in *Claiborne*, strengthens the position of all those who wish to use boycotts as a means of political protest. It is interesting, though, that in all the extensive law review commentary on the *NOW* case, few writers have bothered to discuss the parallels and contrasts with racial boycotts or the *Claiborne* case.[7]

§6.15 Racial Demonstrations Since the Sit-In Period: Recent Cases

Though times have changed, and the Movement may have exchanged more radical means for mainstream efforts, parades and marches remain popular methods of expressing and publicizing political views. And, a generation after the beginning of the civil rights era, some local governments still at-

6. *See, e.g.*, R. Kennedy, *Political Boycotts, the Sherman Act, and the First Amendment: an Accommodation of Competing Interests*, 55 S. Cal. L. Rev. 983 (1982); Comment, *Application of the Sherman Act to Politically Motivated Boycotts—Missouri v. National Organization for Women, Inc.*, 1981 Ut. L. Rev. 599 (1981); Note, *Convention Boycotts - Ruled Outside the Purview of the Sherman Act: Missouri vs. the National Organization for Women (N.O.W.)*, 7 So. Univ. L. Rev. 263 (1981); Note, *The Sherman Act is Inapplicable to a Politically Motivated but Economically Tooled Boycott Where Anticompetitive Methods Abut the First Amendment Right to Petition the Government*, 30 Drake L. Rev. 383 (1980-81).

All of these articles discuss the *NOW* case extensively without mentioning racial boycotts or the *Claiborne* case. Though the Supreme Court decision in *Claiborne* had not been announced when some of these articles were written, the Port Gibson boycott and litigation had received substantial publicity for several years.

7. One of the few law review articles that has addressed the Port Gibson boycott at any length is Note, *Constitutional Rights of Noncommercial Boycotters: A Delicate Balance*, 10 Hofstra L. Rev. 773 (1982). The note discusses political boycotts in general, devoting about equal time to the Port Gibson and NOW boycotts. Written before the Supreme Court decision in *Claiborne*, the note seems to accept the Mississippi Supreme Court's characterization of the Port Gibson boycott as tainted by violence and coercion. The author argues that though political boycotts are protected by the First Amendment, merchants should be given more protection against secondary or violent boycotts.

The *Claiborne* case is mentioned briefly in two notes analyzing the NOW boycott: *Commercial Entities and Political Boycotts: First Amendment Protections versus Sherman Act Prohibitions*, 14 Conn. L. Rev. 391 (1982), and *NOW or Never: Is There Antitrust Liability for Noncommercial Boycotts?* 80 Colum. L. Rev. 1317 (1980).

tempt to prevent or control such public demonstrations. Though the federal courts have consistently, if not always strongly, upheld the rights of public speech and expression, the definition of speech or expression protected by the First Amendment and the limits of a municipality's quite valid power to maintain public order are still being addressed by the federal courts.

A pair of recent cases from Mississippi illustrate this process. In *Beckerman v. City of Tupelo*,[8] InCAR (International Committee Against Racism) challenged several municipal ordinances regulating parades and sound equipment. The ordinances included provisions (1) authorizing denial of parade permits if the chief of police determined that issuance would probably cause injury to persons or property or provoke disorderly conduct, (2) banning permits after 6:00 p.m., (3) requiring marchers to stay in one lane of travel and maintain intervals of 15 feet between units, (4) requiring that participants conduct themselves in an orderly manner and use no profanity, and (5) banning the use of sound equipment in residential zones and between 6:00 p.m. and 9:00 a.m. In practice, the city's application of the ordinances was selective, with exceptions made for activities by governmental agencies and by students participating in educational activities.[9] The district court upheld the ordinances, but the Fifth Circuit reversed, finding all but one of the ordinances unconstitutionally vague, overbroad, and a prior restraint on freedom of speech. The exception was a provision requiring that applicants for permits demonstrate anticipated noise levels.

In *Robinson v. Stovall*,[10] members of the United League challenged a similar set of ordinances in Okolona, Mississippi. During the summer of 1978 the small town of Okolona was the site of a series of United League marches and rallies protesting local racial discrimination and unfair law enforcement. Hostile white groups, including the Ku Klux Klan and the White Citizens Council, staged marches of their own. To control this situation, the Okolona Board of Aldermen adopted ordinances requiring marchers to obtain permits prior to each march, to maintain an interval of one yard between participants, and to assemble and commence the march within 30 minutes of the scheduled starting time. After the ordinance was adopted there were no further marches by white groups. The United League obtained permits for and carried out several marches, though maintaining that the 30 minute rule was impossible to observe.[11]

The next spring, city authorities informed the League that the entire ordinance would be enforced strictly and proceeded to revoke permits of marches on April 14 and 28 because they did not begin promptly. Almost 300 marchers were arrested on these two occasions. Members of the United

8. 664 F.2d 502 (5th Cir. 1981).
9. *Id.* at 506.
10. 646 F.2d 1087 (5th Cir. 1981).
11. *Id.* at 1088.

League promptly filed suit challenging the ordinances and seeking an injunction against their enforcement, but the district court dismissed, holding that the interests of the plaintiffs who had not been arrested were so "intertwined" with those of the plaintiffs who were arrested that the *Younger* doctrine of equitable restraint barred relief as to either class.[12] On appeal, the Fifth Circuit reversed the dismissal, holding that the class of plaintiffs who had not been arrested could seek appropriate injunctive and declaratory relief without any obstacles from the *Younger* doctrine. The court stated that except in extraordinary circumstances a civil rights plaintiff's ability to sue to vindicate his or her right in federal court is not affected by simultaneous pendency of state prosecution against someone else, distinguishing the *Younger* situation where a federal plaintiff seeks directly to enjoin state prosecution. The case was remanded for a hearing on the merits.[13]

In a recent decision, *United States v. Grace*,[14] the United States Supreme Court did a little housekeeping of its own. The Court overturned a federal statute that prohibited the "display [of] any flag, banner, or device designed or adapted to bring into public notice any party, organization, or movement" in the Supreme Court building or on its grounds.[15] The statute included the public sidewalks adjacent to the Supreme Court building in its definition of "grounds." A picketer who carried a sign containing the text of the First Amendment and a person distributing handbills concerning oppression in Central America challenged the statute after being asked to leave the sidewalk by Court police officers. The Supreme Court held that public sidewalks are traditionally considered to be public forums and though the government may enforce reasonable time, place, and manner regulations, it could not constitutionally prevent exercise of First Amendment expressive activities such as peaceful picketing and distribution of leafletts.[16]

§6.16.1 More on Protests Involving the Flag

Though long recognized as rich in symbolic content, protests involving the American flag remain likely to provoke reprisals from employers and bystanders and hostile reactions from the courts. In *Leonard v. City of Columbus*,[17] black policemen who were improperly discharged after demonstrations that included removing an United States flag patch from their uniforms sued for wrongful discharge and reinstatement, only to have their

12. *Id.* at 1090.
13. *Id.*
14. 103 U.S. 1702 (1983).
15. 40 U.S.C. §13k (1976 & Supp. V 1981).
16. 103 U.S. at 1710.
17. 705 F.2d 1299 (11th Cir. 1983).

suit dismissed by the District Court for the Middle District of Georgia. On appeal the Eleventh Circuit recognized that the flag incident constituted symbolic speech which is protected under the First and Fourteenth Amendments and granted the officers a chance to try their case.[18]

Leonard stemmed from an incident in 1971 when black policemen, protesting discriminatory practices within the force and by police officers in the treatment of black citizens, formed an "Afro-American Patrolmen's League" and submitted a list of complaints and requests to the police department. After attempts to pursue the matter with department officials failed, black officers began to picket the police station in a peaceful and orderly manner. At a meeting with civic leaders the officers agreed to cease picketing, but when police officials violated this "cooling down period," League members resumed picketing and removed the American flag patch from their uniforms, announcing that they could not wear it because of injustice on the force. Subsequently, the officers were discharged on the grounds that their removal of an official part of their uniforms was conduct unbecoming officers. After their discharge other reasons were given, including "making baseless allegations of racism and discrimination" and violating police regulations regarding demonstrations.[19]

The Eleventh Circuit found that the League Members' dismissal did not follow established Columbus procedures, and that though many officers neglected to wear the flag patch, no police officer had been disciplined for this infraction before the League incident. Apparently, up to that time, few Columbus policemen had been aware of a 1969 directive making the flag an official part of the uniform. From these facts the court concluded that the officers were dismissed less for the act of removing the flag patch than for the symbolic meaning expressed by that action.[20]

Unorthodox dress or behavior in minorities is also likely to lead to hostile reactions. In *Kolender v. Lawson*[21] the United States Supreme Court held unconstitutional a section of the California Penal Code that required persons who loiter or wander on the streets to provide "credible and reliable" identification when asked to do so by a police officer. Justice O'Connor's opinion held that the statute violated the standards of due process by vesting complete discretion in the hands of the police to determine what a suspect must do to provide "credible and reliable" identification.[22] The opinion will necessitate rewriting of such statutes, but it is not the sweeping decision, allowing citizens to refuse to identify themselves to the police, that the plaintiff sought.[23] Though not addressed in the opinion,

18. *Id.* at 1302.
19. *Id.* at 1301.
20. *Id.* at 1306.
21. 103 S. Ct. 1855 (1983).
22. *Id.* at 1860.
23. *Newsweek*, May 16, 1983, p. 63.

media coverage of the case stressed the disproportionate use of such statutes to stop and question members of minority groups.[24] The plaintiff, Edward Lawson, is a black man who wears his hair in "dreadlocks" and likes to take long walks at night. He challenged the statute after he had been arrested 15 times, prosecuted twice, and convicted once for refusing to identify himself.[25]

§6.21 Protest Rights in Residential Areas: Carey v. Brown

An Illinois statute prohibiting residential picketing was struck down by the Supreme Court in *Carey v. Brown*.[26] The Court held that the statute was "constitutionally indistinguishable" from the one invalidated in *Police Department of Chicago v. Mosley*[27] and that by exempting picketing involving a labor dispute, it impermissibly discriminated between lawful and unlawful conduct based upon the content of the demonstrator's communication. The controversy arose when members of the Committee Against Racism participated in a peaceful demonstration on the public sidewalk in front of the home of Chicago Mayor Michael Bilandic to protest his failure to support the busing of school children to achieve integration. The picketers were arrested and charged with unlawful residential picketing in violation of Illinois statutes.[28]

Though similar statutes have consistently been overturned,[29] it is important to note that the cases do not support any substantive right to picket or demonstrate in residential areas. In the *Carey* opinion the Supreme Court cautions, "[w]e are not to be understood to imply, however, that residential picketing is beyond the reach of uniform and nondiscriminatory regulation."[30] The opinion goes on to discuss the state's high interest in protecting the well-being, tranquility, and privacy of the home. But as with earlier reassurances of this kind,[31] the Court provided no guidelines as to how all residential picketing might be banned without violating federal statutes authorizing picketing when a labor dispute is involved.

24. *See, e.g., Time*, May 16, 1983.
25. 103 S. Ct. at 1856.
26. 447 U.S. 455 (1980), *aff'g* Brown v. Scott, 602 F.2d 791 (1979).
27. 408 U.S. 92 (1972). The Illinois provisions involved were Ill. Rev. Stat., ch. 38, §21.1-2.
28. 447 U.S. at 460.
29. *See also* People Acting Through Community Effort v. Doorley, 468 F.2d 1143 (1st Cir. 1972).
30. 447 U.S. at 466.
31. *See* Gregory v. City of Chicago, 394 U.S. 111 (1969).

§6.22 *Protest Rights in Shopping Centers: Using State Constitutions*

Though *Lloyd Corp Ltd. v. Tanner*[32] remains the leading case construing First Amendment rights in privately owned shopping centers, the movement to interpret state constitutional provisions independently of the federal constitution has produced some interesting developments in this area.[33] In *Pruneyard Shopping Center v. Robins*[34] the United States Supreme Court upheld a California decision finding a right of free speech and petition on shopping center premises based on provisions of the California constitution.[35] Though the federal constitution does not create individual First Amendment rights of expression in privately owned shopping malls, the reasoning in *Lloyd* does not limit the authority of the states to adopt more expansive individual liberties in their constitutions. The Court held that the creation of such a right of access does not constitute an unconstitutional infringement of the shopping center owner's property rights.[36]

Several states, in their own constitutions, have followed California's lead and created a right of free speech and petition on private premises that are held open to the public. Washington and Connecticut have followed the *Pruneyard* approach in regard to petitioning activities in shopping centers.[37] New Jersey and Pennsylvania have extended the theory to public events held on private university campuses.[38] The New Jersey Supreme Court opinion in *State v. Schmid* has a particularly good discussion of the private property owner's right to fashion reasonable rules to control the mode, opportunity, and site of such protected expression.[39] California has applied the *Pruneyard* approach in numerous situations, including the distribution of informational leafletts by a prisoner's rights group in a prison parking lot.[40]

32. 407 U.S. 551 (1972).

33. For another example of this movement, see Chapter 5, §5.16 for the *Wheeler* and *Soares* rules in peremptory challenge cases.

34. 447 U.S. 74 (1980).

35. Robins v. Pruneyard Shopping Center, 23 Cal. 3d 899, 153 Cal. Rptr. 854 (1979).

36. 447 U.S. at 81.

37. Alderwood Associates v. Washington Environmental Council, 635 P.2d 108 (Wash. 1981); Cologne v. Westfarms Associates, 37 Conn. Sup. 90, 442 A.2d 477 (Conn. Sup. 1982).

38. State v. Schmid, 84 N.J. 535, 423 A.2d 615 (N.J. 1980); Commonwealth v. Tate, 432 A.2d 1382 (Pa. 1981).

39. 423 A.2d at 630.

40. Prisoners Union v. Cal. Dept. of Correction, 135 Cal. App. 3d 930, 185 Cal. Rptr. 634 (1982).

Part III
Facsimiles of Rights for Basic Needs

Chapter 7
The Quest for Effective Public Schools

§7.6.4 The 1980 Term: Dissenting from the Denials of Certiorari

The Supreme Court in its 1980 term continued to sidestep the racial balance remedy issue. The writs of certiorari in the *Dallas* litigation were dismissed as improvidently granted.[1] Justice Powell filed a dissenting opinion joined by Justices Stewart and Rehnquist. The dissenters believed the time was ripe to reexamine the considerations relevant to framing equitable remedies in the school desegregation arena.[2]

In *Tasby v. Estes*,[3] the district court found that the decline in Anglo enrollment in the Dallas public schools, from 69 percent of the total enrollment in 1971 to 33.5 percent in 1979, was not the result of actions taken by the school board. A remedy calling for racial balance no longer seemed feasible; instead the district court sought a plan that would achieve the maximum desegregation possible in light of these demographic changes. The plan approved by the district court, however, left 62 of the district's 172 schools with "one-race" student populations (those schools where one race accounted for more than 75 percent of the student body). Most of the one-race schools resulted from the district court's reluctance to order busing of very young children. The court likewise declined to order busing of high school students in the 1976 order — although 1,000 Anglo students had been ordered transported to minority high schools under the 1971 Dallas desegregation plan, fewer than 50 Anglo students attended those schools in 1976.

1. *See* Second Edition §7.6.3.
2. 444 U.S. 437, 438 (1980).
3. 412 F. Supp. 1185 (N.D. Tex 1977).

The Fifth Circuit Court of Appeals remanded the 1976 desegregation plan with orders to formulate a revised plan.[4] Additionally, the district court was called upon to issue findings to justify the maintenance of any one-race schools under the new plan. This was the posture of the *Dallas* litigation when certiorari was granted by the Supreme Court in 1979.

In his dissent from the dismissal of the writ of certiorari, Justice Powell claimed the Fifth Circuit had failed to accord proper deference to the district court in view of that court's greater familiarity with Dallas and its schools.[5] Focusing on the changing demographics and, by implication, the role that the 1971 desegregation plan had played in the population shifts, Justice Powell decried the "continued imposition of self-defeating remedies."[6]

To at least three members of the Court it was increasingly evident that "use of the busing remedy to achieve racial balance can conflict with the goals of equal educational opportunity and quality schools."[7] The dissenters questioned judicial authority to impose racial balance remedies arguably in excess of any constitutional violation attributable to the affected school authorities. Particularly in large cities, they viewed segregated schools as an immutable result of residential segregation over which school authorities exercised no control.

Thus, in the 1980 term, the Court was split as to how far a remedy might go without undermining the uneasy racial balances that had been achieved in earlier desegregation orders. As early as 1971, the Court had expressed the view that "[t]he measure of any desegregation plan is its effectiveness." *Davis v. School Commrs. of Mobile County*.[8] Almost a decade later, the issue was no longer desegregation; the focus was on resegregation. The courts had earlier acted to remove the effects of purposeful segregation. Justice Powell now warned against "the danger of inciting resegregation by unduly disrupting the public schools."[9]

That self-defeating remedies had become the unintended legacy of the pursuit of racial balance continued to trouble at least four Justices throughout the 1980 term. In *Cleveland Board of Education v. Reed*,[10] Justice Rehnquist wrote the dissent from the denial of certiorari. His opinion, which was joined by the Chief Justice and by Justice Powell, drew heavily on the earlier dissent in the *Dallas* litigation.

The petitioners in *Reed* sought to present two issues for review in the Supreme Court: whether the district court had properly found systemwide segregative intent on the part of the Cleveland school board; and whether

4. 572 F.2d 1010 (5th Cir. 1978).
5. 444 U.S. 437, 438 (1980).
6. *Id.* at 439.
7. *Id.* at 438.
8. 402 U.S. 33, 37 (1971).
9. 444 U.S. at 444.
10. 607 F.2d 714 (6th Cir. 1979), *cert. denied*, 445 U.S. 935 (1980).

the systemwide reassignment plan ordered by the district court — a plan which required every grade in every school to have a racial balance in approximate proportion to the systemwide ratio of black to white students — exceeded the scope of the violation shown, particularly in light of the evidence that Cleveland's residential areas are highly segregated by race.

Justice Rehnquist believed that a review of the Cleveland remedy was warranted. In his opinion, the district court had overstepped its authority by imposing such a harsh remedy. Conceding that there was a systemwide constitutional violation, Justice Rehnquist sought to admonish the district court that racial balance was not constitutionally required to remedy the violation. According to Justice Rehnquist the remedy ordered in Cleveland was not sufficiently related to the violation. The district court's discretion, he averred, "did not extend to restructuring the entire demography of the city of Cleveland as reflected in its schools, unless that demography was attributable to the conduct of the petitioner school board."[11]

As the 1980 term progressed, it became increasingly evident that residential demographic changes were undermining the ability of the district courts to order narrowly tailored desegregation plans. In *Alexis I. DuPont School District v. Evans*,[12] petitioners sought a writ of certiorari to review the propriety of a district court remedy which dissolved 11 independent school boards and created a single county-wide school system to be run by court-appointed officials for a period of five years. The Court denied this petition as well. This time Justice Rehnquist was joined by Justices Stewart and Powell.

Referring to the county-wide remedy as "draconian,"[13] Justice Rehnquist questioned its propriety, even while accepting as settled the finding of an interdistrict violation which warranted the imposition of an interdistrict remedy. Particularly troubling to Justice Rehnquist was the abolition of governmental entities that had not been purposeful participants in the constitutional violation.[14] The district court attributed much of the school attendance pattern to shifting residential patterns over the past two decades. The housing patterns were not attributable solely, or even principally, to any governmental actions. Relying on the traditional equitable notion that the remedy should restore the status quo, Justice Rehnquist could not abide a remedy based on the questionable assumption that but for systemwide segregative actions on the part of the local school boards, county neighborhoods would reflect precise racial parity.[15]

Although the Supreme Court declined to address the propriety of racial balance remedies during its 1980 term, the dissents pointed out what

11. 445 U.S. at 937-938.
12. 446 U.S. 923 (1980).
13. *Id.* at 923.
14. *Id.* at 925-926.
15. *Id.* at 927-928.

was becoming increasingly obvious to school officials and local courts: "that perfect solutions may be unattainable in the context of the demographic, geographic, and sociological complexities of modern urban communities."[16]

Increased private school enrollments, continued "white flight" to suburban areas, and refusals to move into school districts all have contributed to resegregation of urban schools. Once such resegregation has been effected in the absence of state action, the courts are stripped of their power to impose additional remedies. Furthermore, when economically advantaged families flee the cities, tax bases shrink and city services suffer. Despite the Supreme Court's apparent resegregation remedies, it is clear that new remedies are necessary if the efficacy of any desegregation plan is to be judged not by its effectiveness in abolishing segregative intent on the part of school authorities, but rather by its effectiveness in creating a stable, racially-balanced educational system.

§7.6.5 The 1981 Term: The Threat of Referenda

On June 30, 1982 the Supreme Court announced its decisions in *Crawford v. Board of Education of the City of Los Angeles,*[17] and a companion case, *Washington v. Seattle School District No. 1.*[18] Each case involved a struggle for control between a duly-constituted local school board with a program for busing to achieve integration and the statewide electorate. In each case a statewide referendum had been passed to terminate the use of mandatory student busing to achieve racial balance. The Supreme Court struck down the Washington law as a violation of the equal protection clause of the Fourteenth Amendment, but upheld the California initiative.

The "Seattle Plan" and Initiative 350. In 1978, Seattle, Washington, School District No. 1 enacted the "Seattle Plan" to achieve racial balance in its schools.[19] The plan made extensive use of mandatory pupil assignment and busing to schools outside the students' immediate neighborhood. These provisions were necessary because residential segregation in Seattle and the

16. 444 U.S. at 448.
17. 458 U.S. 527 (1982).
18. 458 U.S. 457 (1982).
19. The Seattle school board defined racial imbalance as the situation which existed in any school where the combined minority student enrollment exceeded the district-wide combined minority average of 20 percentage points; no school was to have a single minority group enrollment in excess of 50 percent of the student body. Washington v. Seattle School District No. 1, 473 F. Supp. 996, 1006 (W.D. Wash. 1979).

proportion of minorities in the school system[20] were such that racial imbalances could not be corrected through voluntary desegregation techniques.

United in their opposition to the Plan, a group of Seattle residents formally chartered the Citizens for Voluntary Integration Committee, CiVIC, on January 16, 1978. CiVIC's first efforts were directed at obtaining injunctive relief against the Plan's implementation. When these efforts failed, CiVIC drafted a statewide referendum (Initiative 350) to terminate the use of mandatory busing to achieve racial integration of Washington schools.[21]

Initiative 350, which received a 66 percent favorable vote state-wide at the November 1978 general election, required a judicial declaration of a constitutional duty to desegregate before any school board could assign a student to a school, other than the student's nearest or next nearest school, for racial balancing purposes. A number of provisions, however, preserved the power of local school authorities to assign students away from their nearest schools for a panoply of nonintegrative reasons.[22] Believing that

20. The public school population of Seattle School District No.1 is approximately 54,000 students; 37.3 percent of these students belong to racial minorities.

21. Only three of the state's 300 school districts were busing students to achieve racial balance at the time Initiative 350 was proposed. These three districts, Seattle, Tacoma, and Pasco had a combined student population of 88,500 during the 1978-1979 school year — no more than 15,000 of these students were being bused to achieve racial parity. Overall, school districts across the State of Washington bused some 285,000 additional students during the 1978-1979 school year for reasons unrelated to race. Seattle School District No. 1 v. State of Washington, 473 F. Supp. 996 (W.D. Wash. 1979).

22. Initiative 350 provided, in full:

> Section 1. Notwithstanding any other provision of law, after the effective date of this act no school board, school district, educational service district, or county committee, nor the superintendent of public instruction, nor the state board of education, nor any of their respective employees, agents or delegates shall directly or indirectly require any student to attend a school other than the school which is geographically nearest or next nearest the student's place of residence and which offers the course of study pursued by such student, except in the following instances:
>
> 1. If a student requires special education, care or guidance, he may be assigned and transported to the school offering courses or facilities for such special education, care or guidance;
> 2. If there are health or safety hazards, either natural or man made, or physical barriers or obstacles, either natural or man made, between the student's place of residence and the nearest or next nearest school; or
> 3. If the school nearest or next nearest to his place of residence is unfit or inadequate because of overcrowding, unsafe conditions or lack of physical facilities.
>
> Section 2. In every such instance where a student is assigned and transported to a school other than the one nearest his place of residence, he shall be assigned and transported to the next geographically nearest school with the

forbidding mandatory student assignments for race-related reasons while allowing such assignments for virtually any other reason created an impermissible racial classification in violation of the Fourteenth Amendment, the Seattle School District raised a constitutional challenge to the initiative in federal court. The district court agreed that Initiative 350 impermissibly created racial classification that could not be justified by any compelling state interest.[23] In light of this constitutional infirmity, the district court permanently enjoined enforcement of the initiative. It was of no moment to the district court that Initiative 350 made no explicit mention of race;[24] the net result was disallowance of student assignment for racial reasons, which was found to deny equal protection, regardless of how it was achieved.[25]

---

necessary an applicable courses and facilities within the school district of his or her residence.

Section 3. For purposes of section 1 of this act, "indirectly require any student to attend a school other than the school which is geographically nearest or next nearest the student's place of residence within the school district of his or her residence and which offers the course of study pursued by such student" includes, but is not limited to, implementing, continuing, pursuing, maintaining or operating any plan involving (1) the redefining of attendance zones; (2) feeder schools; (3) the reorganization of the grade structure of the schools; (4) the pairing of schools; (5) the merging of schools; (6) the clustering of schools; or (7) any other combination of grade restructuring, pairing, merging or clustering: PROVIDED, That nothing in this chapter shall limit the authority of any school district to close school facilities.

Section 4. For the purposes of section 1 of this act "special education, care and guidance" includes the education, care or guidance of students who are physically, mentally or emotionally handicapped.

Section 5. The prohibitions of this chapter shall not preclude the establishment of schools offering specialized or enriched educational programs which students may voluntarily choose to attend, or of any other voluntary option offered to students.

Section 6. This chapter shall not prevent any court of competent jurisdiction from adjudicating constitutional issues related to the public schools.

Section 7. Sections 1 through 6 of this act are added to chapter 223, Laws of 1969 ex. sess. and shall constitute a new chapter in Title 28A RCW.

Section 8. If any provision of this act, or its application to any person or circumstance is held invalid, the remainder of the act, or the application of the provision to other persons or circumstances is not affected.

Compare California Proposition I, set forth *infra*, note 37.

23. 473 F. Supp. 996, 1011 (W.D. Wash. 1979).

24. See note 4 *supra.*

25. The district court also rested its holding on two additional grounds. The court noted first that racially discriminatory intent was a motivating factor in the adoption of Initiative 350. The court also commented that Initiative 350 was unconstitutionally overbroad because it prohibited mandatory student assignment plans even where school districts may have been under an unlitigated constitutional duty to eliminate *de jure* segregation. 473 F. Supp. at 1011.

The Ninth Circuit Court of Appeals affirmed,[26] agreeing that Initiative 350 embodied a constitutionally suspect classification, and thus was invalid unless the classification provided the least drastic means to achieve some compelling state interest.[27] The court rejected the state of Washington's argument that Initiative 350 was a simple change in the law and could have no constitutional implications without proof of discriminatory intent.[28] It found more than a simple repeal or modification was involved in the Washington case, where a different governmental body — the statewide electorate — had acted to abrogate the power of a duly constituted local school board already subject to local political control.[29]

On writ of certiorari, the Supreme Court affirmed. Justice Blackmun, writing for a 5-4 majority,[30] found that Initiative 350 worked an unconstitutional reallocation of of political power. He commented:

> [T]he political majority may generally restructure the political process to place obstacles in the path of everyone seeking to secure the benefits of governmental action. But a different analysis is required when the state allocates governmental power non-neutrally, by explicitly using the *racial* nature of a decision to determine the decision-making process.[31]

Use of the racial nature of the issue to define the decision-making process, Blackmun continued, impermissibly imposed "substantial and unique burdens on racial minorities." Although the state electorate could have vested all control over education at the state level, the electorate could not constitutionally choose to treat busing for racial purposes differently from all other educational issues.

It was this *shift* in decision-making authority, from local school board autonomy to state-wide control in racial balance issues, that set Initiative 350 apart from California's Proposition I.[32] By singling out the racially conscious issue of busing for distinct, and arguably disadvantageous, political treatment, Washington voters had gone beyond "the simple repeal or

26. *See* §7.6.4 *supra*, official rescission of a previously adopted desegregation technique was permissible in the absence of an antecedent constitutional duty to eliminate *de jure* segregation.

27. 633 F.2d 1338 (9th Cir. 1980).

28. The Ninth Circuit found it unnecessary to review either the district court's holding that Initiative 350 was born of the discriminatory animus of the state electorate, or the district court's conclusion that Initiative 350 was unconstitutionally overbroad.

29. This became the critical distinction between Initiative 350 (Washington) and Proposition I (California), as well.

30. 458 U.S. 527 (1982). Justice Blackmun's opinion was joined by Justices Brennan, White, Marshall, and Stevens.

31. *Id.* at 470. (emphasis in original).

32. *See California's Proposition I infra.*

modification of desegregation or anti-discrimination laws."[33] Having once chosen to operate through local school boards, the state was bound to do so within the confines of the equal protection clause of the Fourteenth Amendment — and its core principle that unjustified distinctions based on race cannot be countered.

Justice Powell, writing for the minority,[34] expressed vehement disapproval of the Court's "unprecedented intrusion into the structure of a state government."[35] Powell read Initiative 350 as creating a policy of strict racial neutrality in school assignments. He found nothing offensive to the Fourteenth Amendment in a preference for neighborhood schools, and a decision not to assign students on the basis of race. Most troubling to the dissent was the question of when, if ever, a state would be able to adopt a racially neutral policy to replace a voluntarily adopted race-conscious remedy:

> The Court's decision intrudes deeply into normal State decision-making. Under its holding the people of the State of Washington apparently are forever barred from developing a different policy on mandatory busing where a School District previously has adopted one of its own . . . . After today's decision it is unclear whether the State may set policy in any area of race relations where a local government body arguably has done "more" than the Fourteenth Amendment.[36]

California's Proposition I. The challenge to Proposition I, which provides that California state courts shall not order mandatory pupil assignment or transportation except to remedy a federal constitutional violation,[37]

33. Crawford v. Board of Education of the City of Los Angeles, 458 U.S. 527, 539 (1982).

34. Justice Powell's dissent was joined by Chief Justice Burger, and Justices Rehnquist and O'Connor.

35. 458 U.S. at 489.

36. *Id.* at 499 n.14.

37. Since ratification of Proposition I, section 7 of the California Constitution reads, in relevant part:

> (a) A person may not be deprived of life, liberty, or property without due process of law or denied equal protection of the laws; provided, that nothing contained herein or elsewhere in this Constitution imposes upon the State of California or any public entity, board, or official any obligations or responsibilities which exceed those imposed by the Equal Protection Clause of the Fourteenth Amendment to the United States Constitution with respect to the use of pupil school assignment or pupil transportation. In enforcing this subdivision or any other provision of this Constitution, no court of this state may impose upon the State of California or any public entity, board, or official any obligation or responsibility with respect to the use of pupil school assignment or pupil transportation, (1) except to remedy a specific violation of the Equal Protection Clause of the Fourteenth Amendment to the United States Constitution, and (2) unless a federal court would be permitted under federal decisional law to impose that obligation or responsibility upon such party to remedy the specific

was decided by the Supreme Court on the same day as the *Seattle* decision. The validity of Proposition I was raised in the context of the desegregation of Los Angeles schools, in the case of *Crawford v. Board of Education of the City of Los Angeles.*[38]

Litigation to desegregate the Los Angeles schools began in 1963 with the filing of a class action suit on behalf of minority students.[39] Seven years later, a California trial court found that the Los Angeles school system had been segregated in violation of both the state and federal constitutions. The school board was directed to submit a desegregation plan for immediate implementation.

The initial decision of the trial court found *de jure* segregation in violation of the Fourteenth Amendment, as well as *de facto* segregation, which alone was sufficient to make out a violation of the California Constitution. On appeal, however, the California Supreme Court based its affirmance solely on the trial court's finding that the state constitution had been violated; the 1970 finding of *de jure* segregation received no appellate imprimatur.

The Los Angeles Board of Education initially submitted a predominantly voluntary desegregation plan for the trial court's approval. The trial court rejected this plan, however, substituting a desegregation plan that called for substantial mandatory student reassignment and transportation along racial and ethnic lines. This desegregation plan, which took effect at the commencement of the 1978-1979 school year, was grounded in the California Constitution's requirement that state school boards take reasonable steps to eliminate *de facto*, as well as *de jure*, segregation.

In November of 1979, the California statewide electorate ratified Proposition I, an amendment to the California Constitution which eliminated the power of California state courts to order mandatory student transportation as a remedy for *de facto* segregation. Under Proposition I, the power of the state courts to mandate pupil reassignment and transportation is coex-

---

violation of the Equal Protection Clause of the Fourteenth Amendment to the United States Constitution.

Nothing herein shall prohibit the governing board of a school district from voluntarily continuing or commencing a school integration plan after the effective date of this subdivision as amended.

In amending this subdivision, the Legislature and people of the State of California find and declare that this amendment is necessary to serve compelling public interests, including those of making the most effective use of the limited financial resources now and prospectively available to support public education, maximizing the educational opportunities and protecting the health and safety of all public school pupils, enhancing the ability of parents to participate in the educational process, preserving harmony and tranquility in this state and its public schools, preventing the waste of scarce fuel resources, and protecting the environment.

38. 458 U.S. 527 (1982).
39. *Id.* at 529.

tensive with the power of the federal courts — no involuntary desegregation plan can be ordered in the absence of a finding of *de jure* segregation violative of the Equal Protection Clause of the Fourteenth Amendment.

The passage of Proposition I coincided with strong dissatisfaction over the Los Angeles desegregation plan, which had then been in effect for one year.[40] Following the election, the school district moved in the trial court for an end to all mandatory reassignment and busing. This motion was denied; the trial court reasoned that Proposition I could have no force and effect in the *Crawford* litigation, given the trial court's 1970 finding of *de jure* segregation in violation of the Fourteenth Amendment.

On appeal, the California Court of Appeals reversed. Initially, the California appellate court found that the 1970 finding of *de jure* segregation could not support a conclusion that there had been intentional segregation in violation of the federal constitution.[41] Moreover, the California Court of Appeals could find nothing constitutionally objectionable about the proposition. Accordingly, the court of appeals vacated the orders entered by the trial court. The California Supreme Court denied review, but the United States Supreme Court granted certiorari.

The Supreme Court upheld the constitutional validity of Proposition I. The state constitutional amendment did not employ any racial classification on its face, so there was no need to demonstrate a compelling state interest. Even if Proposition I was assumed to have an adverse impact on minorities, the Court found no reason to take issue with the conclusion of the California court that no discriminatory animus had motivated the state's voters in their approval of the proposition. Thus, the Court was left with "the simple repeal" of a desegregation or anti-discrimination law. The Court commented that "[i]t would be paradoxical to conclude that by adopting the Equal Protection Clause of the Fourteenth Amendment, the voters of the state thereby had violated it."[42]

Justice Blackmun concurred, but wrote separately to highlight the distinction between Proposition I and Washington's Initiative 350.[43] In Blackmun's view, Initiative 350 had worked an impermissible structural change in the political process which would make it more difficult for certain racial and religious minorities to achieve legislation in their interest. Because Proposition I did not reallocate decision-making authority, but merely limited the power of the state court to deal with desegregation cases, there was no constitutional infirmity.

40. This dissatisfaction was shared by all parties to the *Crawford* litigation, *see id.*

41. This conclusion followed from the changing standards expressed by the United States Supreme Court during the 1970's in those cases where discriminatory intent was at issue. *See, e.g.*, Washington v. Davis, Second Edition §9.8, and Village of Arlington Heights, Second Edition §8.15.2.

42. 458 U.S. at 535.

43. *Id.* at 545.

Justice Marshall could not agree. Dissenting, he pointed out that the distinction between Proposition I — which limited the power of the judiciary with respect to school desegregation — and Initiative 350 — which reallocated decision-making authority with respect to the same issue — was insufficient to justify the different results in *Crawford* and *Seattle*.

Justice Marshall searched the record for a compelling state interest to justify the discriminatory reallocation of governmental decision-making authority that he believed to be at issue in both *Crawford* and *Seattle*, but could find none. Furthermore, Marshall disagreed with the Court's blind acceptance of the state court's conclusory statements as to whether discriminatory intent had played any role in the adoption of Proposition I.

Finally, Justice Marshall noted that Proposition I was in some sense "better" than the Washington initiative struck down in *Seattle* because under the California law those seeking racial balance remain free to petition school officials for voluntary compliance with the continuing state constitutional duty to desegregate. Nevertheless, Marshall added, the California voters had deprived minorities of "the only method of redress that has proven effective — the full remedial powers of the state judiciary."[44]

§7.8.4 Tasby v. Wright

After the Supreme Court decided, after two terms, that certiorari should not have been granted (see §7.6.4 *supra*), the *Dallas* school case was returned once again to the district court where Judge Barefoot Sanders, following a month-long hearing, issued a lengthy opinion finding that while "vestiges of state-imposed racial segregation" remained, "systemwide transportation is not a feasible remedy for the existing constitutional violation."[45] A number of intervening groups had joined the case, including the NAACP, supporting the original plaintiffs who claimed the 1976 plan had not gone far enough to remedy past segregation, and the Black Coalition to Maximize Education (Black Coalition). They produced a large number of witnesses who convinced the court of the wide difference of opinion within Dallas's minority community as to the appropriate relief in the case. They proved, the court said, that no longer could one party speak for the entire minority population as a "sacrosanct 'class.' "[46]

44. *Id.* at 562.

45. Tasby v. Wright, 520 F. Supp. 683, 686 (N.D. Tex. 1981).

46. The court described the Black Coalition as "a broad-based minority community group composed of parents, patrons and taxpayers with children in the DISD, as well as representatives from a number of civic, political and ecumenical associations in the black community." 520 F. Supp. at 689. The groups included the Dallas Urban League, Black Chamber of Commerce, Council of Black Parents,

The court reviewed in great detail the demographic changes in the school district whose school population was 49.6 percent black, 19.4 percent Hispanic, and 29.5 percent Anglo. He noted that the minority population had almost doubled since 1970, acknowledged the large number of whites who had moved from the district, but denied that fear of "white flight" would bar effective relief. "That does not mean," Judge Sanders said, "that the Court must ignore the unpleasant realities of population changes as it devises a plan."[47]

The focus of attack during the hearing was East Oak Cliff, an area of some 21 square miles and serving 25,000 mainly black students, which had been designated as one of six subdistricts in the 1976 plan. The original plaintiffs and the NAACP urged that further desegregation could be obtained with other subdistricts or with the largely white suburbs surrounding the Dallas school district. They pointed to the fact that two Anglo and 77 minority schools were essentially one-race schools (90 percent either Anglo or minority), and were undeterred by the overall racial make-up requiring designation of any school of no more than 75 percent Anglo or minority population as a desegregated school.

The Board maintained that a racial balance plan able to achieve this goal had been found impractical because of the great distances involved (the district covers some 351 square miles) and the concomitant expense. The Black Coalition also contended that black parents in the East Oak Cliff district were opposed to a busing plan because their schools were performing well and their children achieving at higher levels than were minority students attending racially balanced schools.[48]

Judge Sanders evidenced particular concern about the difficulties of busing children in the first three grades for distances requiring an hour or more ride each way, the hardships involved, and the growing disenchantment in the black communities in other urban school cases, including Atlanta, Boston, and Nashville, with traditional racial balance remedies.[49]

Black Business and Professional Women, the National Council of Women (Dallas Section), and the Dallas Ministerial Alliance.

47. 520 F. Supp. at 700.

48. East Oak Cliff is not a typical black ghetto. From an undeveloped area in the 1950's, its housing was constructed by a series of subdivision developments for whites. New schools, streets, parks, and shopping centers were built. Then in a three-year period in the 1960's, the area changed from an almost entirely white residential area to a primarily black area.

49. Principles of fair disclosure require pointing out that the court's opinion quotes at several places the work of this editor, including D. Bell, *Serving Two Masters: Integration Ideals and Client Interests in School Desegregation Litigation*, 85 Yale L.J. 470 (1976), at footnotes 11, 12, and text at 732, which page also cites D. Bell, *Brown v. Board of Education and the Interest-Convergence Dilemma*, 93 Harv. L. Rev. 518 (1980).

The editor has also visited Dallas on two occasions serving as a consultant to the East Oak Cliff district of the Dallas school system. He has met with black com-

On this point, he quoted from the trial testimony of Dallas school board president Kathyrn Gilliam, one of three minority members, who in the judge's words "described the perception of busing in the black community in compelling terms":[50]

> I don't think that additional busing is even the issue . . . it has never been the issue. . . . [T]he issue is whether or not we are going to educate the children and youth. I think that the whole question around the whole busing issue just loses sight of why we are here and what the schools are about now. I think it was a noble idea in 1954 . . . but what I envisioned and I'm sure what other black parents envisioned in 1954 just never happened.[51]

Based on testimony of black and Hispanic parents that their desegregation experience in Dallas had been "both traumatic and unproductive," Judge Sanders said "the imposition of mandatory transportation on minority parents and children who are opposed to such a remedy is unfair and paternalistic." Parents complained of hostile school environments and the negative implications of minority neighborhood inferiority and loss of self esteem by minority children implied by busing them to Anglo schools. Particular concern was expressed about the damage to small children resulting from school assignments far from home. The court found that independent factors of time and distance made busing an inappropriate remedy, but the vigorous opposition expressed by minority parents was "another factor which weighs in the scales of equity against the feasibility of *Swann* transportation remedies."[52]

Applying these standards to the virtually all-black East Oak Cliff district, Judge Sanders found no basis to change the conclusion in the 1976 court order that the subdistrict was beyond the reach of effective desegregation tools, but that steps should be taken to afford equal educational opportunity to all students. Citing the Supreme Court's *Milliken v. Bradley* decision,[53] he found the Dallas district had made real progress in eliminating educational inequalities inherent in the dual school system.[54]

---

munity leaders and recommended community organization and intervention in the litigation.

50. 520 F. Supp. at 732.

51. *Id.*

52. *Id.* at 733.

53. Milliken v. Bradley II, 433 U.S. 267 (1967).

54. The court reported:

> Under the semi-autonomous direction of Dr. Yvonne Ewell, a noted black educator, and an extensive central office staff, the East Oak Cliff subdistrict has developed a unique educational program for the students within its boundaries designed (1) to ensure mastery of the basic academic and social skills; (2) to develop a multi-cultural curriculum and school environment; and (3) to encourage parental and community involvement with the school. Support for the

The court observed that academic debate had intensified about the extent of educational benefits realized by children as a result of integrated education. Plaintiffs' expert testified that minority children would achieve best where the concentration is below 50 percent minority, a fact the court found of little relevance in a system where the minority population is over 70 percent. Minority students in East Oak Cliff and other one-race minority schools all were able to gain admission to more integrated schools under the Board's majority to minority transfer plan as well as the series of magnet school programs placed in operation as part of the desegregation plan.

In a subsequent hearing, Judge Sanders was called on to determine the validity of a Minority Neighborhood Option Plan (MNOP) filed by the Board at the request of minority parents (not living in East Oak Park) unhappy with racial balance remedies for grades 4-6 and 7-8 under the 1976 plan. The revised plan would enable minority parents to opt out of their right to have their children bused to an integrated school. The MNOP plan was opposed by the NAACP and supported by the Black Coalition.

The court saw merit in the concept, but felt constraints imposed by Fifth Circuit precedent rendered the plan unacceptable. Operation of the plan, the court feared, would lead to a resegregation of the schools. "On the other hand," Judge Sanders suggested, "the Court believes that in the proper circumstances basic rules of equity may soon force a shift in these long accepted legal principles to accommodate the growing disagreement in minority communities over the nature of desegregation relief."[55] But, the court concluded, the MNOP has potential. "The 27 years since *Brown I* have exacted a toll on the traditional goals of school desegregation litiga-

---

effort to develop a more responsive educational system for black children has been forthcoming from the school district which has allocated an additional $1 million over each of the last several years for East Oak Cliff. . . .

The model of instruction developed in East Oak Cliff, praised and emulated by leading educational authorities across the country, rests on the basic assumption that minority children have the equal ability to learn and can learn, if necessary, in a predominantly minority setting. The success of these educational components can be traced in the steady and significant upward trend in achievement levels for black students in all basic skills areas since the implementation of the 1976 court order and the creation of the subdistrict. Between 1976 and 1980, for example, the percentile rankings for reading achievement in grade 2 rose from 26 to 52, an increase mirrored in tests of language arts and mathematics. Similar improvement was documented in grades 4, 6 and 8 although the degree of achievement is generally much lower with each grade above K-3. The improvement in East Oak Cliff schools appears to be occurring more in the lower grades, considered to be the most efficient and lasting method of comprehensive educational change.

Minority achievement in EOC, furthermore, has increased as much or more than minority achievement in the rest of the school district . . .

520 F. Supp. at 741-742 (footnotes omitted).

55. Tasby v. Wright, 542 F. Supp. 134 (N.D. Tex. 1982).

tion; the remedies designed for the 1980's may have to be dramatically different from those developed in the past."[56]

As to the present, the court determined that "improvement of student achievement, especially minority student achievement, must be the priority effort for the District."[57] To this end, Judge Sanders ordered the board to make an annual allocation of $50 per minority student attending a mainly minority school, and set a formula that would provide additional teachers for students functioning below the 30th percentile.[58]

In what was apparently a premature hope "that this seemingly endless legal struggle which actually began in 1955, . . . can soon be brought to an end. . . ." Judge Sanders in a 1982 order awarded plaintiffs' attorneys $391,578 in fees and expenses of $30,305.[59] As in so much school desegregation litigation, it again appears that the lawyers handling the case for both sides are the only clear winners. Those they represent are left with more expectations than genuine relief. That the prospects for blacks in East Oak Cliff are more hopeful than most is as much the result of self-help efforts as the all too rare sensitivity to the situation exhibited by the district court.

§7.8.5 The Trend Toward Education Remedies in School Desegregation Cases

The transition from a racial balance to an effective education-oriented relief pattern in the *Dallas* case is dramatic, but an examination of on-going litigation in several other school cases reveals similar patterns. In some cases though, school board interest in quality education in black schools is motivated, at least in part, by the continued opposition of whites to desegregated schools.

Little Rock, Arkansas, site of major school desegregation confrontations in the late 1950's, is a not surprising example of this trend. There, the

56. *Id.* Judge Sanders supported his prediction with the suggestion that proponents of the MNOP must address the issues of equal protection for whites not afforded a waiver, and the impact of the plan on minority students who choose not to exercise the waiver provided them under the plan.

57. 542 F. Supp. at 134.

58. Judge Sanders's orders were generally upheld on appeal. Tasby v. Wright, 713 F.2d 90 (5th Cir. 1983). His finding that the Dallas system had not achieved unitary status withstood school board objections as did his rejection of the Minority Neighborhood Option Plan (MNOP). The black parent groups who introduced the plan did not appeal, but the school board did. The Fifth Circuit did find that because so few students would be affected, and that more natural desegregation would occur in a year or two, Judge Sanders had abused his discretion in altering school board lines in East Dallas so as to provide some desegregation in a few all-white schools.

59. Tasby v. Wright, 550 F. Supp. 262 (N.D. Tex. 1982).

court of appeals affirmed a district court approved plan even though it created four virtually all-black schools and reduced the black enrollment in five schools located in white or integrated neighborhoods (although none below 50 percent). As a result, about 19 percent of all nonwhite elementary school students were placed in racially identifiable schools. All white students would attend fully integrated schools, and all students in black schools were given an option of transferring to an integrated school with transportation provided by the school district.[60]

In 1973, the Little Rock system served 21,095 students, 48 percent black; by 1981, only 18,104 students remained in the system, and 65 percent were black. The Board found that some whites moved to the suburbs to avoid desegregation, and that the black population had increased because of a higher birth rate. The city's boundaries expanded, but not those of the school district because it could not get approval of outside districts. Forty percent of the city is now outside the boundaries of the district. The Board issued reports on this in 1980.[61] Over the years, several efforts have been made to appease white parents. Some have been struck down by courts.

The plan adopted by the Board is based in part, on recommendations by the federal government's School Desegregation Assistance Team that urged steps to improve achievement levels of black students.[62] Approval by the court of appeals of the plan was conditioned on Board implementation of provisions "to make sure that black students have equal educational opportunities."[63]

The school district's administration recommended that the district strive to achieve the following characteristics in the four all-black schools: "a climate of expectation in which no child is permitted to fall below minimum standards; an environment that is orderly without being rigid, quiet without being oppressive; an emphasis on the acquisition of basic school skills over other school activities; the flexibility to divert school energy and resources from other business in furtherance of the fundamental objectives; and the existence of procedures to monitor frequently pupil progress."[64]

60. Clark v. Board of Educ. of Little Rock School Dist., 705 F.2d 265 (1983).

61. *Id.* at 266-267.

62. *Id.* at 268.

63. 705 F.2d at 272-273. The court cited *Milliken II*, Andrew Jackson High School v. Ambach, 598 F.2d 705, n.3 (2d Cir.); and Evans v. Buchanan, 582 F.2d 750, 767-769 (3d Cir. 1978).

64. 705 F.2d at 272, n.13. See also, Kelley v. Metropolitan Co. Board of Educ. of Nashville and Davidson Co., Tenn., 687 F.2d 814 (6th Cir. 1982), *cert. denied*, 459 U.S. 1183 (1983). While requiring a *Swann*-type racial balance plan, the court affirmed on the basis of *Milliken II* educational components "for those schools or classes where the achievement levels are below the average for the system and/or where the majority of a school's population is made up largely of socio-economically deprived children who suffer the continuing effects of prior discrimination." *Id.* at 816-817. The court also approved an Afro-American studies program over plaintiffs' objections to lack of specificity of such programs. 687 F.2d at 817.

Finally, the long-running legal/political battle over school desegregation in Chicago has reached another, but likely not the last, plateau with a district court's approval of a far-reaching plan that relies heavily on educational improvement rather than racial balance and busing.[65] In approving the school board's plan over the NAACP's objections, the court noted that the suit started with a consent decree. Litigation, the court admonished plaintiffs, should have been filed many years ago when the possibility existed for far more desegregation than is now possible. Moreover, the court cited the fact that the Board had appointed a nationally known black expert in school desegregation, Dr. Robert Green, who had come up with comprehensive set of educational components, all of which the Board adopted.[66]

As to the student assignment plan, the court said that in the last ten years, the total school population has shrunk by 25 percent, to some 435,000, and racial make up had changed drastically. Whites went from 34.6 percent in 1970-71 to 16.3 percent in 1982-83. Blacks went from 54.8 percent to 60.7 percent and Hispanics from 9.7 percent to 20.4 percent. Still, the court found, "Essentially, the NAACP's contention is one for racial balance in all schools."[67] Instead of reliance on busing, the Board opted for a plan of voluntary transfers and mandatory measures other than transportation to bring about the greatest number of stably integrated schools. The Board preferred the neighborhood concept and pointed to a survey showing busing would lead to more "white flight."[68] The court cited experiences in Los Angeles, Boston, and Detroit showing that busing causes between 40 percent and 45 percent of white students to leave the system. The Board could not refuse to act because of a fear of white flight, but said, "Once within the range of constitutionally permissible desegregation plans, however, the Board was free to choose one calculated to minimize parent resistance and thereby serve its larger goal."[69]

§7.12.5 Affirmative Action Since Bakke

There have been few significant judicial developments in educational affirmative action since the *Bakke* decision in 1978. Universities and professional schools continue, with more or less vigor, to conduct minority admissions programs, despite periodic challenges by excluded white applicants. Most of these seem to be without much merit, as in the case of

65. United States v. Board of Educ. of Chicago, 554 F. Supp. 912 (N.D. Ill. 1983).
66. *Id.* at 915.
67. *Id.* at 923.
68. *Id.* at 924.
69. *Id.* at 925.

Doherty v. Rutgers School of Law,[70] where a white male applicant was excluded because of consistently low grades and entrance exam scores. At the opposite end of the spectrum is *Marquez v. University of Washington,*[71] which upheld the termination of a Hispanic law student who had been on probation for two years. The Washington Supreme Court noted wryly that the law school had provided this student with informal tutoring and assistance and was not required to create a formal minority assistance program for his benefit.[72] Though affirmative action in education, as in employment, remains vulnerable to constitutional challenge, no really well-conceived challenge has been reported.[73]

§7.13.6 Black Colleges and the Desegregation Dilemma

In *Mississippi University for Women v. Hogan,*[74] the Supreme Court held that an all female nursing school's refusal to admit males was unconstitutional. The Court rejected defendant's argument that the all female school is necessary to compensate for women's past disadvantage in the job market, noting that nursing has traditionally been dominated by women. The opinion indicated, however, that in areas where women have suffered discrimination, such as business and the professions, a single sex school might be justifiable. There are obvious parallels to the dilemma of all black colleges. Since blacks have suffered discrimination in every field of employment, *Mississippi University* provides a useful rationale to show that there is a continuing need for all black colleges.

70. 651 F.2d 893 (3d Cir. 1981). A similar case is DeRonde v. Regents of the University of California, 28 Cal. 3d 875 (1981), *modifying* 101 Cal. App. 3d 221 (1980).

71. 97 Wash. 2d 1037, 648 P.2d 94, *cert. denied,* 460 U.S. 1013 (1983).

72. 97 Wash. 2d at 1040, 648 P.2d at 97.

73. *See* discussion in Second Edition, §9.11.4. For further reading in this area, *see* Brooks, *Affirmative Action in Law Teaching,* 14 Col. Hum. Rights L. Rev. 15 (1982).

74. 458 U.S. 718 (1982).

Chapter 8
Property Barriers and Fair Housing Laws

§8.1.1 *Housing Discrimination in the 1980's*

Discrimination in housing, with its vices of segregated housing patterns and inadequate and overpriced housing for minorities, continues to be one of those areas where the law is unable or unwilling to keep up with conditions in the real world. Despite the multiplicity of federal and state statutes designed to deal with housing discrimination, the law is not structured to provide effective relief. Most state statutes, like the federal Fair Housing Act,[1] are not self enforcing, but rely on implementation by overburdened agencies or injured individuals who typically have few resources. Given the rather tame sanctions contained in the FHA, and the traditionally low damage awards in housing discrimination suits, the existing law serves neither to discourage wrongdoers nor compensate the injured.[2]

Housing laws and agencies are even less well suited to deal with the complicated issues that surround urban renewal and low-income housing projects where the parties are not individuals but municipalities, agencies, and large classes of affected citizens. The difficulty of fashioning plans to effectively break up segregated housing patterns and provide low income housing is exacerbated by the ease with which legal tactics and dilatory ploys can be used by opponents to thwart them.

Despite this pessimistic assessment of the existing laws, the potential exists to make these laws the framework for more effective enforcement. The impetus for enforcement, however, lies with a strong public desire for change, recognized and supported by the government and the courts. The

1. Fair Housing Act of 1968, 42 U.S.C. §§3601-3619 (1976 & Supp. IV 1981)(also known as Title VIII).

2. For a recent evaluation of the effectiveness of the FHA, *see* Lamb, *Congress, the Courts, and Civil Rights: The Fair Housing Act of 1968 Revisited,* 27 Vill. Law Rev. 1115 (1982). The article faults the Act's weak, uncentralized enforcement powers for its lack of effectiveness, and notes that amendments to rectify these problems were introduced unsuccessfully in Congress in 1979 and 1980. *Id.* at 1140.

Reagan administration, from 1980 to 1984, placed little emphasis on enforcing the existing laws and less on developing the law into an effective means of change. One of the sadder ironies of the past few years is the widespread view that in a time of recession, when aid is most desperately needed, the United States cannot afford to fund social programs. This apparent expression of the truism that in hard economic times there is less to go around, becomes a response exposed as a mask for unconcern when viewed in light of recent federal budgets providing for increased military spending and tax breaks for the wealthy. The effect of cuts in social programs is not to make problems go away, but to shift burdens to the state and local level.

Judicial performance in the housing area has been mixed. The Supreme Court extended standing in FHA housing claims to "testers" and housing organizations,[3] but in another case refused to recognize a street closing between racially defined neighborhoods as either a badge of slavery or diminution of property rights.[4] A skeptic might reconcile the results in these cases by noting that the extension of standing to "testers" is likely to have little practical effect, given the difficulty these parties will have in establishing injury. On the other hand, municipal support of segregated housing patterns is widespread, and a successful challenge in Memphis could have led to devastating results for other cities.

A wide spectrum of approaches can be found in the lower and state courts. In cases concerning individuals a number of decisions support more generous awards of damages and attorney fees than have been common in housing suits.[5] At the same time, a number of courts, both state and federal, continue to rule on damages in ways that are not only ungenerous but wrong.[6] Such diverse results highlight the inefficiency of the case by case method of combatting discrimination. Yet those who seek to bring larger controversies before the courts, such as segregated housing patterns and opposition to public housing, find that their task is no easier. The checkered career of the *Gautreaux* litigation,[7] to name just one of the cases that has been in the courts for many years, shows that the judicial forum can be more effectively used by those who seek to delay change than those who seek to implement it. There have been some stirrings of judicial impatience with such tactics, like the remarks of the New Jersey Supreme Court in the most recent Mt. Laurel case, vowing to put some teeth into their decision

3. Havens Realty Co. v. Coleman, 455 U.S. 363 (1982). *See* discussion in §8.9 *infra.*

4. City of Memphis v. Greene, 451 U.S. 100 (1981). *See* discussion in §8.4 *infra.*

5. *See, e.g.,* McDonald v. Verble, 622 F.2d 1227 (6th Cir. 1980); Shaw v. Cassar, 558 F. Supp. 303 (E.D. Mich. 1983).

6. *See, e.g.,* Woods-Drake v. Lundy, 667 F.2d 1198 (5th Cir. 1982); Phillips v. Hunter Trails Community Association, 685 F.2d 184 (7th Cir. 1982); Marable v. Walker, 704 F.2d 1219 (11th Cir. 1983).

7. *See* §8.13.4 *infra* for discussion of the ongoing *Gautreaux* controversy.

this time.[8] However, such isolated examples of judicial commitment do not compensate for inadequate and ineffective national policy.

§8.4.3 *Section 1982 and the Thirteenth Amendment*

In the late 1970's the City of Memphis, at the request of a group of white neighbors, decided to restrict the volume of traffic on a street leading into city center by closing the street at the point where the white neighborhood ended and a largely black neighborhood began. The decision was not part of a city-wide traffic control program, and was in fact the first residential street closure in Memphis. The closure was accomplished by deeding a strip of land across the street to the white neighborhood association. The effect was to restrict black access to the white neighborhood, and to require residents of the black neighborhood to take an alternate route to city center. Residents of the black neighborhood filed a class action under the Thirteenth Amendment and 42 U.S.C. §1982, charging that the barrier's creation of racially separate neighborhoods was a "badge of slavery," and that it reduced property values in the black community for the benefit of the white neighborhood.[9]

The district court found that the street closing did not create a benefit for white citizens which was denied black citizens, that the city had not departed significantly from normal procedures in authorizing the closing, and that racially discriminatory intent had not been proved.[10] The Sixth Circuit reversed, holding that the trial court had limited its inquiry too severely, and that though a street closing may be a legitimate means of dealing with traffic flow, §1982 and the Thirteenth Amendment dictate relief when the effect of an action is to create racially separate neighborhoods. The appeals court called the placement of the barrier at the dividing line between the neighborhoods highly suspicious and ruled that it would depreciate property values in the black area.[11]

The Supreme Court granted certiorari to investigate the standard of intent required to show discrimination under §1982 and the Thirteenth Amendment, but found it unnecessary to reach that issue, holding that black citizens did not suffer a significant property injury by the closure.[12]

8. Southern Burlington County NAACP v. Mt. Laurel Township, 92 N.J. 158, 456 A.2d 390 (1983).

9. City of Memphis v. Greene, 451 U.S. 100, 102 (1981); 610 F.2d 395, 396-400 (6th Cir. 1979)

10. 451 U.S. at 107-108 (1981).

11. 610 F.2d at 404.

12. Compare the result in Evans v. Tubbe, 657 F.2d 661 (6th Cir. 1981). Evans was one of several landowners who relied on a road running through Tubbe's land to reach their property. Tubbe erected a gate across the road and gave a key to all white landowners but refused to give a key to Evans, who is black. The Sixth Cir-

The closure decision had a legitimate motive, to promote safety and tranquility on residential streets, and black residents suffered only minor inconvenience by being required to use one street rather than another to make certain trips. This, in itself, did not depreciate the value of blacks' property and so could not constitute a badge of slavery.[13] Justice White concurred in the result but would have gone a step further by ruling that proof of discriminatory intent is necessary to establish a cause of action under §1982 and the Thirteenth Amendment.[14]

Justice Marshall, joined by Brennan and Blackmun, dissented strongly, arguing that the court ignored evidence of historic segregation in Memphis, that there was evidence of discriminatory intent in this situation, and that the erection of a barrier to carve out racial enclaves within a city is precisely the kind of injury that §1982 and the Thirteenth Amendment were enacted to prevent. Given the obvious inference of racial motivation that this action raises in anyone familiar with the history of race relations in the city of Memphis, it is facile to attribute the closure simply to a policy decision for valid municipal reasons.[15]

Greene attracted a good deal of comment in the law reviews, and few have found much to commend in it. The gentlest criticisms focus on the Court's failure to establish an intent standard for §1982 and Thirteenth Amendment cases.[16] The decision, the first §1982 case heard by the Court since 1973, represents an ominous retreat from the liberal scope of §1982 envisioned by cases like *Tillman*[17] and *Jones.*[18] Though the opinion did not reach the issue of intent, it seems to set the stage for a requirement of intentional discrimination in §1982 cases.[19] Equally upsetting is the Court's undervaluation of the injury and inconvenience suffered by the black community because of the barrier, and the refusal to take into account evi-

---

cuit held that the maintenance of such a barrier on racial grounds was an incident of slavery under §1982. This may have been an injury of greater magnitude than that in *Greene*, but similar interests were involved.

13. 451 U.S. at 124.

14. *Id.* at 129.

15. *Id.* at 135.

16. Comment, *City of Memphis v. Greene: A Giant Step Backwards in the Area of Civil Rights Enforcement*, 48 Brooklyn L. Rev. 621, 622 (1982).

17. Tillman v. Wheaton-Haven Recreational Association Inc., 410 U.S. 431 (1973).

18. Jones v. Alfred H. Mayer Co., 392 U.S. 409 (1968). *See also*, Note, *Civil Rights — Racial Discrimination and Property Rights — the Scope of 42 U.S.C. §1982*, 29 Wayne L. Rev. 203 (Fall, 1982).

19. Comment, *Dead-end Street: Discrimination, the Thirteenth Amendment, and Section 1982, City of Memphis v. Greene*, 58 Chi.-Kent L. Rev. 873, 904 (1982). The Comment analyzes *Washington v. Davis, Arlington Heights,* and *Greene* as a trio representing a shift away from broad construction of the Civil Rights Act of 1866.

dence of historic[20] and contemporary[21] discrimination by the city of Memphis. As one commentator put it, the *Greene* decision may become the "prototype of facially neutral actions used as smokescreens to cloak discrimination."[22]

The Supreme Court seems to have decided not that there was no injury to black residents, but, as in so many other areas of racial conflict, including electoral districts, seniority policies, and educational testing, that such injury must be borne if it arguably can be explained on some racially neutral ground. Even when, as in *Greene,* the discriminatory intent seems palpable, one reads an unspoken concern that, some other time, in some other case, blacks might be able to thwart some legitimate municipal policy decision because of its adverse impact on them. It is this fear and the complex, unspoken but generally accepted reasoning out of which the fear emanates, that poses a barrier to racial equality that is far more massive than anything erected on a Memphis city street.

§8.7.1 Damages for Intangible Injury, and Other Damages Issues

Most housing cases, like *City of Memphis v. Greene,* involve large numbers of people and difficult public policy decisions. Often, inequities result not only from individual acts of discrimination, but from historical patterns of segregation and neglect. Though such controversies are most effectively dealt with at the municipal, state, or national level rather than by litigation between individuals, the bulk of housing litigation is brought by private parties under the Fair Housing Act.[23] Despite a full range of private remedies for individual acts of discriminationin the sale or rental of housing,[24] many courts still experience difficulty in applying the FHA to private claims. The uncertainty of any remedy, coupled with the traditionally low damages granted in housing cases, ensure that the private enforcement mechanisms of the FHA are unlikely to become an effective substitute for publicly initiated action.

As an example, which sadly is not isolated, of the difficulty courts have in applying housing discrimination law, consider the case of *Woods-Drake*

20. *Id.* at 895.

21. Casenote, *Constitutional Law — Civil Rights — Memphis Street Closing: Minimal Inconvenience or Monument to Racial Hostility?,* 22 Santa Clara L. Rev. 931, 941 (1982).

22. 48 Brooklyn L. Rev. at 641.

23. For a critical analysis of the FHA's strengths and weaknesses see, Lamb, *Congress, the Courts, and Civil Rights: The Fair Housing Act of 1968 Revisited,* 27 Vill. Law Rev. 1115 (1982).

24. Fair Housing Act of 1968, 42 U.S.C. §§3601-3619 (1976 & Supp. IV 1981).

v. Lundy.[25] The plaintiffs, a white clergyman and his wife, were evicted from their apartment for entertaining black guests. The trial judge found that the landlord had threatened to evict the plaintiffs if they continued to receive black guests, and that their lease had been terminated for that reason. Nonetheless, the judge found the defendant not liable under the FHA, §1981 or §1982, speculating that the landlord may also have had other reasons for the eviction. The judge also held that the plaintiffs sustained no compensable damages, though they had been forced to move to a more expensive apartment, and that punitive damages would not be in order since the landlord had not been "vindictive."[26]

On appeal the Fifth Circuit ruled that reversal was clearly compelled under both §1982 and the FHA since racial animus need only be a substantial factor, not the sole motivation for a discriminatory action. The Fifth Circuit sternly instructed the trial court to award both compensatory and punitive damages on remand, noting that in the first trial plaintiffs had submitted an itemized list of their moving costs. The court also noted that "being old and set in his ways" was not sufficient to excuse the defendant landlord from punitive damages when the record showed that he had used racial expletives in threatening the Woods-Drakes and had a history of racially motivated evictions.[27]

In *McDonald v. Verble,*[28] another recent case, an owner and realtor evaded showing a piece of property to a black man interested in purchasing it, and rejected his offer for the amount they were asking. After plaintiff filed suit and got a restraining order on sale of the property, the owner sold it to him. At trial the judge held that purchase of the property was the plaintiff's sole remedy, and that since he had no further claim the case was dismissed with costs for the defendants. The Sixth Circuit remanded, instructing the trial court that the opportunity to buy the property, coerced by the injunction and pending suit, did not fully compensate the plaintiff for the original act of discrimination, and that even without this continuing claim, the defendants could not be held to have prevailed at the trial level.[29]

The *Woods-Drake* and *McDonald* cases are not isolated incidents. Judicial misunderstanding of the most basic concepts of the FHA, at least at the trial level, is so widespread that plaintiffs bringing even simple housing complaints must be prepared to follow the case to the appellate level, in effect making every housing case a test case. Not only does this discourage plaintiffs from using the existing laws, the uncertainty inherent in such claims discourages defendants from settling before trial. One of the most common errors in claims brought under more than one statute is confusion

25. 667 F.2d 1198 (5th Cir. 1982).
26. *Id.* at 1202.
27. *Id.* at 1203.
28. 622 F.2d 1227 (6th Cir. 1980).
29. *Id.* at 1233.

over the allowable damages. Courts frequently limit punitive damages granted for §1982 claims to $1,000, although that limitation applies only to FHA claims.[30] The trend in recent appellate decisions has been to disapprove any implied limitation on punitive damages in non-FHA housing suits.[31]

Damages granted to blacks for emotional harm caused by housing discrimination continue to be less generous than those granted routinely in other civil suits, but there are some indications of growing judicial sensitivity to the presence and seriousness of emotional injury in housing cases.[32] The Kentucky Supreme Court recently upheld the power of an administrative agency to award damages for emotional injury caused by housing discrimination, stating that humiliation and embarassment lie at the core of the evil that the Kentucky Civil Rights Act was designed to eradicate.[33] Even in less sensitive jurisdictions, plaintiffs may be able to generate higher damage awards by coupling common law tort or other statutory claims with claims under fair housing statutes.[34]

A growing number of courts are willing to grant damages for emotional distress and humiliation without evidence of medical treatment for physical manifestations of the emotional harm.[35] In *Marable v. Walker*,[36] the Eleventh Circuit held that emotional injury could be inferred from the plaintiff's testimony that the defendant mocked his desire to live in a white section of town and hung up the telephone on him. However, a number of courts still treat emotional injury claims with the suspicion voiced by the

30. *See* Marable v. Walker, 704 F.2d 1219 (11th Cir. 1983) (trial court fixed punitive damages at $1,000 for §1982 claim; remanded also for evidentiary hearing on emotional damages and attorney fees); Phillips v. Hunter Trails Community Assoc., 685 F.2d 184, 191 (7th Cir. 1982) (award of $100,000 in punitive damages under §1982 affirmed).

31. Woods-Drake v. Lundy, 667 F.2d 1198, 1204 (5th Cir. 1982).

32. For instance, in Phillips v. Hunter Trails Community Association, 685 F.2d 184 (7th Cir. 1982), a wealthy black couple was granted $10,000 each for humiliation and emotional distress after they were prevented from moving into an exclusive neighborhood. The court noted that this was the highest award it had seen for emotional damages, and that most awards have ranged from $500 to $5,000. *Id.* at 190. *See also* Kushner, *Fair Housing: Discrimination in Real Estate, Community Development and Revitalization* 478 (1983)(table of damages awarded in housing discrimination cases).

33. Kentucky Commission on Human Rights v. Barbour, 625 S.W.2d 860 (Ky. 1981).

34. *See, e.g.*, Shaw v. Cassar, 558 F. Supp. 303 (E.D. Mich. 1983) (claim brought under Michigan anti-lockout statute and Michigan fair housing act by couple locked out of newly rented apartment; the court awarded damages of $15,000 each for emotional distress and humiliation).

35. *Damages for Embarrassment and Humiliation in Discrimination Cases II*, Kentucky Commission on Human Rights, Staff Report 82-88 (1982).

36. 704 F.2d 1219 (11th Cir. 1983).

district court in *Nicholson v. Bates*: "such intangible injuries are manifestly indeterminate and involve inherent uncertainty."[37]

One tool that could be used more creatively in private housing discrimination suits is injunctive relief, but trial courts are typically conservative in fashioning remedies in these cases. The Eleventh Circuit approved the district court's order in *Marable v. Walker*,[38] which enjoined the defendant from applying disparate criteria based on race in renting apartments, but suggested that the injunction should go further and require the defendant to rent plaintiff an apartment as well. In *McHaney v. Spears*,[39] where real estate developers attempted to rescind a sales contract for a building lot after learning that the buyers were black, the court ordered specific performance of the contract. These are not radical decisions, and are consistent with traditional remedies in transactions concerning land, but unfortunately these cases still represent the exception rather than the rule in housing discrimination cases.

Finally, an important consideration in private housing discrimination claims is the availabilty of attorney fees. Because damage awards have typically been so low, the incentive to pursue legal remedies is diluted even further if attorney fees are unlikely to be awarded. Since the enactment of the Civil Rights Attorney's Fee Act of 1976,[40] federal claimants are better able to predict their chances of securing attorney fees in addition to other damages.[41] In some state courts plaintiffs with meritorious claims still run the risk of bearing their own litigation costs, which may well exceed any award of damages.[42]

37. 544 F. Supp. 256, 258 (E.D. Tex. 1982). This attitude is also seen in the unwillingness of judges and juries to grant damages for emotional harm when no other compensable injury is shown. In *Nicholson* the jury found for the plaintiff, who claimed that defendant had refused to lease an apartment to her, but did not award any damages because no economic injury was alleged, though she had presented evidence of emotional harm. *Id.* at 257.

38. 704 F.2d 1219 (11th Cir. 1983).

39. 526 F. Supp. 566 (W.D. Tenn. 1981).

40. 42 U.S.C.A. §1988 (1983). The Act is discussed in §5.7A of this Supplement.

41. *See* Price v. Pelka, 690 F.2d 98 (6th Cir. 1982); Williams v. City of Fairburn, 640 F.2d 635 (5th Cir. 1981)(plaintiff who obtained desired relief in pre-trial settlement entitled to attorney fees as prevailing party).

42. *See, e.g.*, Miles v. F.E.R.M. Enterprises, Inc., 29 Wa. App. 61, 627 P.2d 564 (1981)(trial court refused to grant attorney fees where jury found that the defendant had discriminated but returned a verdict of no damages).

§8.9.1 More on the "Standing" Issue

Havens Realty Co. v. Coleman,[43] is one of the more significant recent developments in the housing area. In this case, the Supreme Court recognized the standing of housing testers and housing associations to sue in their own right as injured parties. Suit was brought against a realty corporation for racial steering in violation of FHA §804 by one black person (Coles) who had attempted to rent, two testers (one, Coleman, was black, one was white), and HOME (Housing Opportunities Made Equal) a non-profit housing group. The district court dismissed the testers and HOME for lack of standing, trying only Coles's claim. The Fourth Circuit reversed, finding that all plaintiffs made sufficient allegations of injury to have standing, and that the claims were not time barred because based on continuing violations.[44]

The Supreme Court affirmed in part and reversed in part, holding that courts may not create prudential barriers to standing under §812 and that only a minima of injury in fact is required to create standing.[45] By alleging that the realtor misrepresented facts about the availability of housing to him, the black tester gained standing. The white tester could not allege such misrepresentation, and so had no standing to sue.[46] However, both testers had standing to assert that the defendant deprived them, as residents of the community, of the benefits of interracial association.[47] HOME had standing to sue for damages on its own behalf through its claim that steering tactics interfered with its efforts to guide members to integrated housing.[48] The Court also held that the statutory 180-day limit on claims under §804 did not bar the testers' "neighborhood" claims or HOME's injury claim, because these rested on continuing violations.[49] The black tester's misrepresentation claim was held to be barred because the incident occurred more than 180 days before suit was filed.

Havens excited quite a bit of law review comment, some favorable, some critical.[50] Its impact, though, remains to be seen. The decision can be

43. 455 U.S. 363 (1982)

44. Coles v. Havens Realty Corp., 633 F.2d 384 (4th Cir. 1980).

45. 455 U.S. at 371. The Court indicated that it was guided by its decision in Gladstone v. Village of Bellwood, 441 U.S. 91 (1979).

46. 455 U.S. at 375.

47. *Id.* at 377.

48. *Id.* at 378.

49. *Id.* at 380.

50. *See, e.g.,* McRae, *Havens Realty Corp. v. Coleman: Extending Standing in Racial Steering Cases to Housing Associations and Testers,* 22 Urb. L. Ann. 107 (1981) (a very important case with enormous potential significance for racial steering cases and general standing law); Casenote, *Civil Rights — Racial Discrimination — Fair Housing Act of 1968 — Standing for Testers: Havens Realty Corp. v. Coleman,* 21 Duq. L. Rev. 295 (1982) (calls decision an unfortunate broadening of standing requirements which will increase the burden on the courts).

read as an important loosening of standing requirements in racial steering cases. Some commentators have even argued that *Havens* indirectly overrules *Sierra Club v. Morton.*[51] However, it can also be interpreted as a technical holding that will have little practical effect, since, as the opinion notes, it is unlikely that the testers or HOME can show the requisite injury necessary to succeed on the merits.[52] If testers and housing associations can get past standing to prevail on the merits, *Havens* will be confirmed as a potent tool to attack housing practices.[53]

§8.10 Societally Synchronized Housing Remedies: Few Advances

Efforts to remedy housing discrimination in our society fall into two sometimes inconsistent categories: promotion of integrated housing patterns, and provision of better quality housing for members of groups that have suffered discrimination. In the realm of private home sales and rentals the emphasis has been almost exclusively on integration accomplished by removing barriers to entry into "white" neighborhoods.

As discussed in the Second Edition §8.10, integration efforts are made difficult by persistent fears of white residents that black neighbors are, per se, undesirable neighbors whose presence will automatically lower property values and "tip" the character of the area from white to black.[54] Fear of "tipping" is often self-fulfilling, particularly when manipulated by unscrupulous "blockbusters" who use the advent of a single minority family into a neighborhood as a lever to force panic sales by white residents.[55] Even without such wrongful behavior, the psychology of white residents requires a careful study of the dynamics of tipping when formulating and maintain-

51. McRae at 133 (discussing Sierra Club v. Morton, 405 U.S. 727 (1972)).

52. 455 U.S. 363, 377, 379 (1982).

53. NAACP v. Harris, 567 F. Supp. 637 (D. Mass. 1983), followed *Havens* by granting standing to the NAACP for its own alleged injuries in a suit which alleged that HUD failed to prevent discrimination in the administration of federal housing grants. On the merits the court held that although the evidence did not warrant a finding that HUD financed discriminatory programs, the agency had not required the minimum levels of compliance necessary to implement the policy of fair housing of the Civil Rights Act of 1968.

54. The irrationality of such fears is made plain by the reflection that black families, like white families, seek to move into neighborhoods that reflect their income level and their values. Those black families able to move into desirable neighborhoods are likely those with middle-class incomes and tastes.

55. A long-standing shortage of attractive housing for blacks in most urban areas insures that neighborhoods cleared by blockbusting soon find eager black residents. *See* Clark v. Universal Builders, Inc., 706 F.2d 204 (7th Cir. 1983).

ing an integration plan.[56] Care must be taken, however, to distinguish between justifiable fear that a precarious racial balance will be destroyed, and tactics meant to prevent integration.[57]

The danger of theories that cater to white fears is that while they may be a means to promote gradual integration in a few neighborhoods, they provide no principled means of discouraging engrained real estate practices such as racial steering.[58] The difficulty of drawing up statutes to prevent steering without infringing other property rights is illustrated by *Illinois Association of Realtors v. Village of Bellwood*,[59] where two ordinances enacted in an attempt to comply with the *Gladstone* decision[60] were held unconstitutional as vague, overbroad, and a restraint on commercial speech. The statutes required notification of intent to sell or rent residential property and gave the village council discretionary power to license real estate agents.

Similarly the practice of redlining — using boundaries of segregated neighborhoods as criteria in mortgage and loan approval decisions — by financial institutions has proved intractible, despite what one commentator has called "more than enough" state, federal, and local statutes regulating the field.[61] Redlining is particularly invidious because it not only preserves segregated housing patterns, but ensures that development and improvement in minority areas will be difficult to finance.[62]

§8.10.4 Racial Occupancy Controls: Recent Cases

The use of "benign quotas" limiting minority residents in an integrated housing project or neighborhood is a tempting means to counteract white residents' fears and prevent tipping. Though there are a number of concerns raised by any use of quotas that may burden black residents for the

56. *See* Note, *Tipping the Scales of Justice: A Race-Conscious Remedy for Neighborhood Transition*, 90 Yale L.J. 377 (1980).

57. *See, e.g.*, Morris v. Chicago Housing Authority, 500 F. Supp 763 (N.D. Ill. 1980). Residents of an integrated neighborhood in Chicago (over 50 percent white) challenged a plan to build 12 units of low income public housing, claiming that it would "tip" the area. The court held that 12 units of housing were unlikely to change the nature of the area, and refused to enjoin the project.

58. That the real estate industry itself will not act to eliminate racial steering is shown by Sherman Park Community Assoc. v. Wauwatosa Realty Co., 486 F. Supp. 838 (E.D. Wis. 1980), an action brought under §1981, §1982, and the FHA, against Milwaukee area realtors and the local realtors' association, charging that defendants engaged in a pattern of racial steering.

59. 516 F. Supp. 1067 (D. Ill. 1981).

60. Gladstone v. Village of Bellwood, 441 U.S. 91 (1979).

61. Jennings, *Preemption and State Anti-Redlining Regulations: The Need for Clarification*, 11 Fordham Urb. L.J. 225 (1983).

62. *See* Emigrant Savings Bank v. Elan Management Corp., 668 F.2d 671 (2d Cir. 1982).

benefit of whites or that may cause futher exclusion of blacks from housing opportunities,[63] the cases show no coherent pattern. From all indications, the use of benign quotas in housing is still in an experimental period. Several recent federal cases illustrate some of the themes present.

In *Williamsburg Fair Housing Committee v. N.Y.C. Housing Authority*,[64] a housing project's racial quota of 75 percent white, 20 percent Hispanic, and 5 percent black was struck down as arbitrary and not reflective of the racial composition of the area. The court also found that the quotas were administered inconsistently, with frequent deviations to include more white tenants. The case leaves open the questions of what population should be used to set benign quotas, and how close to actual population figures the quotas must come. By contrast, in *Schmidt v. Boston Housing Authority*[65] selection procedures that assigned white, low-income tenants to projects where they would improve the racial balance were approved. In this case, unlike *Williamsburg*, there was no evidence that the procedures were established or administered with any discriminatory intent.

Where the goals of integration and providing better housing for minorities collide, even more difficult issues are raised. In *Burney v. Housing Authority of the County of Beaver*[66] low income blacks on the waiting list for public housing challenged the county's method of filling vacancies. The housing projects in Beaver County reflected its largely segregated housing patterns.[67] Under pressure to integrate, the Housing Authority had divided the County into five districts and filled housing vacancies by giving preference to members of under-represented races in each district, setting a goal of no more than 33 percent black residents in each project. These policies caused a large backlog of blacks on the waiting lists of several mainly black districts. The district court held that although preserving and promoting integration is a legitimate interest under the FHA, benign quotas are impermissible if they restrict black entry into housing more than is necessary to prevent white abandonment.[68] In this case the tipping level of 33 percent was not based upon satisfactory evidence and there were more effective means of integration, such as random county-wide distribution of applicants, that would not burden black residents more heavily than whites.

63. *See* Smolla, *Integration Maintenance: The Unconstitutionality of Benign Programs that Discourage Black Entry to Prevent White Flight*, 1981 Duke L.J. 891 (1981), for a critique of benign quotas.

64. Williamsburg Fair Housing Committee v. N.Y.C. Housing Authority, 493 F. Supp. 1225 (S.D. N.Y. 1980).

65. Schmidt v. Boston Housing Authority, 505 F. Supp. 988 (D.C. Mass. 1981).

66. 551 F. Supp. 746 (W.D. Pa. 1982).

67. *Id.* at 765.

68. *Id.* at 767.

§8.12 Urban Renewal and Black Housing: Private Right of Action Under Title VI and the Community Act

In *Montgomery Improvement Association v. HUD*[69] the Fifth Circuit recognized a private right of action under Title VI and the Community Act[70] to challenge municipal grant recipients' use of federal funds. The plaintiffs accused the city of Montgomery of using block grants to aid homeowners rather than to aid low income and minority residents by eliminating slums and urban blight. The Fifth Circuit held that HUD's enforcement power to terminate or reduce payments to grant recipients who discriminate would not provide the affirmative relief required by the plaintiffs.

§8.13 Public Housing and the Integration Ideology: Acquiescence by Local and Federal Authorities

As *Burney v. Housing Authority of the County of Beaver,*[71] makes clear, the advent of low income public housing did not greatly alleviate residential segregation. Though economic and social factors often militate against integration, it is most disturbing that local and federal agencies, whether intentionally or unwittingly, often assist these impersonal forces in maintaining segregation. For example, a recent case struck down Chickasaw, Alabama's "citizenship" requirement for eligibility for public housing as discriminatory both in intention and in application.[72] The town of Chickasaw, though only five miles from Mobile, Alabama, had no black residents at the time of this suit; though it operated 309 units of public housing, it had never accepted a black tenant. While other housing authorities in the county had hundreds or thousands of applicants on waiting lists, Chickasaw had about 25. Any black applicants for public housing were told that nonresidents weren't eligible, without even being asked if they lived in Chickasaw. In a similar case a class of black residents of public housing in 36 east Texas counties maintained that HUD itself acquiesced in the local housing authorities' maintenance of segregated housing projects.[73]

69. 645 F.2d 291 (5th Cir. 1981).
70. 42 U.S.A. §5301 et seq. (1983).
71. 551 F. Supp. 746 (W.D. Pa. 1982).
72. United States v. Housing Authority of the City of Chickasaw, 504 F. Supp. 716 (S.D. Ala. 1980).
73. Young v. Pierce, 544 F. Supp. 1010 (E.D. Tex. 1982).

§8.13.4 Siting challenges

In *Stryckers Bay Neighborhood Council, Inc. v. Karlen,*[74] the Supreme Court emphasized HUD's discretion in choosing sites for public housing projects. Plaintiffs charged that HUD had improperly changed a Manhattan housing project from middle to low income without considering the project's impact on the surrounding neighborhood under NEPA. The majority held that the HUD had only to affirm that it had considered the project's environmental impact, and that it would not substitute its judgment for that of the agency. Justice Marshall dissented, arguing that the court gave HUD too free a rein.[75] He would have addressed the issue of whether HUD can choose a site that will add to racial and low-income concentration solely because a more desirable site would cause delay.[76]

§8.16 *Exclusionary Zoning Litigation in State Courts:* Mt. Laurel II

In several areas of constitutional and civil rights law, state courts have taken the initiative once reserved to federal courts and agencies. Last year the New Jersey Supreme Court made a valiant effort to attack exclusionary zoning in *Southern Burlington County NAACP v. Mt. Laurel Township.*[77] The case represents the reopening, after eight years, of the *Mt. Laurel* controversy,[78] discussed in the Second Edition §8.16. In response to lower court decisions approving narrow interpretations of the Mt. Laurel doctrine, and minor rezoning and other limited remedies, the New Jersey Supreme Court accepted cases concerning six New Jersey municipalities. The court reiterated its commitment to the *Mt. Laurel* doctrine, and expressed unhappiness with the lack of progress since 1975. Though the doctrine has had some practical effect — numerous New Jersey municipalities have amended ordinances to allow low and moderate income housing — many cases have dragged on in unending litigation.[79]

74. 444 U.S. 223 (1980).

75. *Id.* at 234.

76. The majority approach, however, is favored by the lower courts. *See, e.g.*, Business Assoc. of University City v. Landrieu, 660 F.2d 867 (3d Cir. 1981)(citing *Strykers Bay* as precedent).

77. Southern Burlington County NAACP v. Mt. Laurel Township, 92 N.J. 158, 456 A.2d 390 (1983).

78. Southern Burlington County NAACP v. Township of Mt. Laurel, 67 N.J. 151, 336 A.2d 713, *cert. denied*, 423 U.S. 808 (1975).

79. 92 N.J. at 170, 456 A.2d at 402.

The court put teeth into the *Mt. Laurel* doctrine by recognizing a "builder's remedy" that allows judges to approve increased housing densities if a town's zoning does not provide for a fair share of low and moderate income housing.[80] In addition, incentives are provided to towns that voluntarily rezone in the form of a grace period from builders' suits.[81] Though local reaction to the decision has been mixed,[82] legal commentators have greeted *Mt. Laurel II* as a "landmark" and a major leap in housing law.[83]

80. 456 A.2d at 425.

81. *Id.* at 431.

82. *New York Times*, Feb. 29, 1984. New Jersey's Governor Kean denounced the decision as a "Communist" concept. Officials of several localities indicated that they would give up resistance to low income housing despite continued pressure from local residents. *Id.*

83. *See* Zax and Kayden, *A Landmark in Land Use,* The National Law Journal, March 14, 1983, p.11.

Chapter 9
The Limited Strategy of Fair Employment Laws

§9.1.1 The Current Economic Status of Blacks: 1984

The economic recession that has plagued so many working class Americans in recent years dramatically worsened the employment situation of black Americans. By all reliable measures, the economic status of blacks — a status intimately tied to employment opportunities — has deteriorated at a greater rate than that of whites. The unemployment rate for blacks, always higher than for whites, is now well over twice as high as white unemployment.[1] The unemployment rate for black teenagers has reached new peaks and is still rising.[2] Though white unemployment showed some improvement in 1983, the rate for black workers continued to rise.[3]

The median black family income remains at about 56 percent of white family income, a minimal improvement over 55 percent in 1960.[4] This fig-

1. In 1983 the official unemployment rate for all black workers was 19.5 percent, compared to 8.4 percent for all white workers. U.S. Bureau of Labor Statistics, *Employment and Earnings*, vol. 31, p. 204, Jan. 1984. In 1975 the comparable rates were 13.8 percent for black workers and 7.8 percent for white workers; in 1970, 8.2 percent for black workers and 4.5 percent for white workers. U.S. Bureau of the Census, *1982-83 Statistical Abstract of the United States*, p. 392, Washington, D.C., 1982 ("discouraged" workers not included in official figures).

2. The official unemployment rate for black workers aged 16-19 was 48 percent in 1982 and 48.5 percent in 1983. The rate for white workers aged 16-19 was 20.4 percent in 1982, 19.3 percent in 1983. *Employment and Earnings*, at 204. As recently as 1979 the rate for black teenagers was 35.4 percent. *1982-83 Statistical Abstract*, at 392.

3. White unemployment dropped by .02 percent in 1983, the first annual decrease since 1979. Black unemployment rose .06 percent in 1983. *1982-83 Statistical Abstract*, at 392.

4. *National Review*, Aug. 19, 1983, p.1037. There have been some fluctuations in these figures, including a decrease to 54 percent in 1964, and an increase to 57 percent in 1980. *Black Enterprise*, Jan. 1984, p.34.

ure actually underestimates the degree of black poverty, as the distribution of income among blacks is skewed to a greater degree than among whites, so that the poorest blacks receive a smaller share of total black income than the poorest whites receive of total white income.[5] This may be linked to a shift in the composition of black families in the past two decades. At present, almost half of the black families with children are headed by a single parent (overwhelmingly the mother), compared to 21 percent in 1961.[6] While black families with two parents earn about 80 percent of what similar white families earn, the median income of female-headed black families is less than half that of two parent black families. The median family income for female-headed black families is about $7,500, substantially less than the poverty level for a family of four.[7] As a result, about 46 percent of black children live in poverty.[8] Though white female-headed families are similarly disadvantaged, compared to white two parent families, they comprise only 14 percent of white families.[9]

The net effect of the recession, thus, is not only a freeze in black advancement, but a very real loss of ground. The country's economic woes have had political repercussions as well. The recessions of the past decade have awakened a sense of scarcity, eroding white support for affirmative action, job training, and other social programs that shift resources to minorities and the poor. In the face of high unemployment in all sectors of society, we hear little about creating jobs for minority workers. The Reagan administration's heralded reliance on the private rather than the public sector, in the form of "trickle-down economics," is seen by many as a strategy to maintain the status quo of a white dominated economy. Coupled with the administration's opposition to social programs and affirmative action, its weak civil rights enforcement efforts, and its insensitivity to the realities of poverty and discrimination, it is hard to reach any other conclusion.[10]

5. *Id.* at 36.

6. *National Review*, Aug. 19, 1983, p.1037.

7. *Black Enterprise*, Dec. 1983, p.47 (citing Census Bureau statistics for 1981). The 1981 median family income for black female-headed families was 38 percent of that for black two-parent families. *Id.*

8. *1982-83 Statistical Abstract*, at 442 (1981 figures for children under 16; given greatly increased unemployment in 1982 and 1983, an even higher figure must be posited for those years). Unemployment affects families with children disproportionately: in 1983 42 percent of black families with children did not have even one wage earner. *Employment and Earnings*, at 209.

9. *National Review*, Aug. 19, 1983, p.1037. In 1981 white female-headed families earned about 50 percent of the white two parent family income. *Black Enterprise*, Dec. 1983, p.47. This figure, though distressing, is about $5,000 higher than the 1981 median income of black female-headed families. *Id.*

10. *See Black Enterprise*, Jan. 1984, pp.28, 34 (citing administration's weak enforcement effort, opposition to affirmative action, and reduction of EEOC compliance reviews); *U.S. News and World Report*, July 25, 1983, p.20 (Reagan administration widely criticized as anti-minority).

The black community has responded to this hostile political and economic climate with increased self-reliance and political organization. Black professionals and black-owned businesses, though still underrepresented, are increasing in numbers and visibility.[11] Several major cities have elected black mayors, and for the first time a black presidential candidate has received serious attention.[12] Though such self-reliance cannot take the place of majority support for economic and employment parity, it is preferable to dependence on majority drafted social programs, that have been chronically underfunded, often administered without an understanding of minority concerns, and which for both reasons serve to replace hope with despair and substitute dependency for the basic need: opportunity.

§9.2.4 Sex Discrimination vs. Racial Discrimination

Many significant recent decisions have concerned sexual rather than racial discrimination.[13] While the precedents set by such decisions are often readily applicable in race discrimination cases (and, inevitably, a certain number of cases will involve both classifications), it is appropriate to inquire whether subtle distinctions exist in the analysis of racial and sexual discrimination that may make these decisions not entirely interchangeable as precedents. In Title VII[14] cases, any such distinctions are less immediately apparent than in Fourteenth Amendment analysis, where strict scrutiny is applied to racial but not to sexual classifications, or in §1981,[15] where racial but not sexual discrimination is explicitly prohibited. Both racial and

11. In 1983 about 14 percent of black workers, as opposed to about 24 percent of white workers, held professional or managerial positions. *Employment and Earnings*, at 202. Though blacks are underrepresented in the professions, there has been improvement in the past 15 years. In 1971, 1.9 percent of black workers were lawyers or judges, 6.3 percent were physicians or dentists, 2.6 percent were bank or corporate officers, and 1.3 percent were office or sales managers. In 1981, 4.6 percent were lawyers or judges, 11 percent were physicians or dentists, 5.5 percent were bank or corporate officers, and 4.3 percent were office or sales managers. *1982-83 Statistical Abstract*, at 388. In 1982 there were an estimated 357,000 black-owned businesses in the United States, with a gross income of $16.9 billion. *Black Enterprise*, Jan 1984, p.36.

12. *See* discussion in this Supplement *supra,* §4.1.1. The number of black elected officials in the U.S. has increased from 1,469 in 1970 to 5,606 in 1983. 70 ABA J. 52 (April, 1984). As of March 1984, the Reverend Jesse Jackson was running third in a hotly contested race for the Democratic presidential nomination.

13. *See, e.g.*, Arizona Governing Committee for Tax Deferred Annuity and Deferred Compensation Plans v. Norris, 103 S. Ct. 3492 (1983); County of Washington v. Gunther, 452 U.S. 161 (1981); Texas Dept. of Community Affairs v. Burdine, 450 U.S. 248 (1981).

14. Civil Rights Act of 1964 §§701-718, 42 U.S.C. §§2000e-2000e17 (1976 & Supp. IV 1981).

15. 42 U.S.C. §1981 (1976 & Supp. IV. 1981).

sexual discrimination are targets of Title VII, and the same requirements apply to each classification.

There is a likelihood, however, that the lessened degree of scrutiny accorded to constitutional gender cases may "leak" into Title VII gender cases, causing a practical difference in evaluation of similar facts. There is also the greater occurrence of rational reasons for distinctions between the sexes, based on bona fide occupational qualifications and privacy considerations, whereas there are simply no justifiable reasons for racial discrimination in employment. Finally, society's attitudes concerning appropriate sexual roles and distinctions are less settled and overt than attitudes about racial discrimination, leading to less certainty of discrimination, as a matter of law rather than a matter of proof, in some gender cases. These factors are subtle, and certainly do not negate the great usefulness of gender precedents in racial litigation. What is necessary is an awareness that such attitudes may be present,[16] and that civil rights litigation cannot be treated as monolithic.

§9.3.4 Negotiated Labor Rights vs. Affirmative Action

Some of the thorniest problems in discrimination law today arise from clashes between established labor rights and remedies for past discrimination. Affirmative action plans often conflict with the seniority rights and promotion expectations of white workers.[17] When such plans are mandated by court orders or conciliation agreements, the question arises whether they preempt conflicting collective bargaining provisions. Early cases said not,[18] but the *Weber* decision raised hopes that affirmative action plans might occupy a more favored position than formerly believed. These hopes were weakened by *W. R. Grace & Co. v. Local Union 759*,[19] where the Supreme Court held an employer responsible for a collective bargaining breach caused by its attempt to follow a conciliation agreement in a Title VII suit, and awarded back pay to plaintiff union members.

W. R. Grace & Co. had settled a discrimination claim by adopting an affirmative action plan prohibiting discharge of newly hired minority workers in the event of layoffs. Subsequently, the company ordered layoffs in accordance with the conciliation agreement rather than by strict seniority as provided by the collective bargaining agreement. Union employees filed a

16. For a startling example of the degree to which societal attitudes may color consideration of a gender discrimination case, *see* Hishon v. King and Spalding, 678 F.2d 1022 (11th Cir. 1982), where the court of appeals replied to plaintiff's contention that Title VII applies to law firms' partnership offers with a lengthy comparison of business partnerships to matrimony.

17. *See* §9.11.3.1 on layoffs and seniority rights.

18. *See* Second Edition §9.11.3 for discussion of pre-*Weber* litigation.

19. 103 S. Ct. 2177 (1983).

grievance, and an arbitrator ruled that though the company may have acted in good faith, it had breached the collective bargaining agreement at its own risk, and so was liable.[20] The district court overturned the award on public policy grounds, but the Fifth Circuit reversed and was affirmed by the Supreme Court. The Supreme Court ruled that unless an arbitrator's decision does not draw its essence from the collective bargaining agreement, the reviewing court may not substitute its judgment.[21]

The Supreme Court found that enforcement of the collective bargaining agreement was not contrary to public policy, as it is important to support the established system of labor bargaining and arbitration, and to encourage obedience to judicial orders.[22] The Court stated that Title VII is also an important public policy, and that the company would have been liable for any breaches of the conciliation agreement. However, the Court said Title VII will be best supported by putting the risk and liability in such situations on employers rather than unions.[23] The Court also noted that the employer could have avoided some of its liability by not laying off workers when it did.[24]

It is true that an employer should not remedy its past discrimination at the expense of union workers, but the practical result of this ruling is to encourage employers to choose the support of relatively more powerful unions, and brave employment discrimination claims by minorities. The Supreme Court's opinion does not seriously consider the issues raised by the district court, which held that remediation of the effects of discrimination is so important a public policy that provisions of collective bargaining agreements could be modified in pursuit of that goal.[25]

During negotiations for the conciliation agreement the EEOC invited the union to join in drafting the affirmative action plan, but the union refused to participate.[26] This is an indication that as between the excluded minority workers and the union, the union was to some degree at fault. The history of labor shows that unions as well as employers have fostered racial discrimination.[27] As in other cases, however, the Supreme Court weighed the rights of white employees (who apparently held their positions of se-

20. Facts taken from 652 F.2d 1248 (5th Cir. 1981).

21. 103 S. Ct. at 2182.

22. *Id.* at 2185.

23. *Id.* at 2186.

24. *Id.* at 2184.

25. *Id.* at 2182. The opinion is short and no dissents were filed. Though the case may have significant impact in employment discrimination suits, it is tempting to conclude that the Supreme Court did not really consider the ramifications (explored by the district court) of its decision.

26. *Id.* at 2180.

27. *See, e.g.*, General Building Contractors Assoc., Inc. v. Pennsylvania, 458 U.S. 375 (1982)(union's "hiring hall" practices were racially discriminatory).

niority as the result of past discrimination) as entitled to priority over those of excluded minority workers.[28]

§9.6 *Title VII and Disparate Treatment: New Developments*

Title VII[29] litigation occupied an unusual share of the Supreme Court's attention in the last few terms.[30] However, increased review has not fostered consistent policy, and has left in its wake a confusing mixture of outcomes and principles. The 1983 Term resulted in two more significant rulings on Title VII. The case of *Firefighters Local Union No. 1784 v. Stotts*,[31] presented the recurring theme of the relationship of Title VII to affirmative action plans that conflict with seniority rights (see discussion in §9.11.3).

The other case, *Hishon v. King and Spalding*,[32] decided that Title VII applies to partnership offers by law firms. *Hishon* was brought by a former associate of a large Atlanta law firm who claimed the firm's "up or out" policy is administered discriminatorily. The Eleventh Circuit affirmed dismissal of her claim, ruling that partnerships are not subject to Title VII.[33] Rejecting Hishon's analogy of large law firms to corporate employers, the court emphasized the partnership's freedom of voluntary association.[34]

The Supreme Court, in a decision that could set an important precedent for the many women and minorities who have entered law, only to find that partnership in large firms is still beyond reach, ruled that a law partnership is a benefit of employment within the coverage of Title VII, application of which does not infringe the partners' constitutionally protected rights of expression or association.

Chief Justice Burger, speaking for a surprisingly unified Court, said that if plaintiff could prove that the firm contracted to have her considered

28. *See* Ford Motor Co. v. EEOC, 458 U.S. 219 (1982). *W. R. Grace* has already been followed in a case concerning racial discrimination. EEOC v. Safeway Stores, Inc., 714 F.2d 567 (5th Cir. 1983).

29. Civil Rights Act of 1964 §§701-718, 42 U.S.C. §§2000e — 2000e17 (1976 & Supp. IV 1981).

30. The Court has accepted an unusually high number of employment discrimination and labor relations cases in recent years. In the 1981-82 Term alone, it considered 35 employment related cases, 9 of which directly involved Title VII. *Review of Supreme Court's Term: Labor and Employment Discrimination Law*, 51 USLW 3087 (Aug. 17, 1982). Each term since 1980 has seen at least one significant employment law decision.

31. 104 S. Ct. 2576 (1984).

32. 104 S. Ct. 2229 (1984).

33. 678 F.2d 1022, 1024 (11th Cir. 1982).

34. *Id.* at 1026.

for partnership, that promise is a term, condition, or privilege of employment, and binds the firm to consider her for partnership without regard to her sex. And in only a few brief paragraphs, the Court rejected the firm's contentions that application of Title VII would infringe constitutional rights of expression and association.

While the distinctive contributions lawyers make to the ideas and beliefs of the society were recognized, the Court said the firm had not shown how their ability to fulfill such a function would be inhibited by a requirement that it consider plaintiff for partnership on her merits. And citing several civil rights decisions in the racial area, the Court said "[i]invidious private discrimination may be characterized as a form of exercising freedom of association protected by the First Amendment, but it has never been accorded affirmative constitutional protections."[35]

Most recent cases have concerned procedural or technical elements rather than the substance of Title VII. Few of these decisions were pleasing to civil rights advocates. In *General Telephone Co. of the Southwest v. Falcon*,[36] the Court severely tightened certification requirements in Title VII class actions, ruling that a Hispanic employee passed over for promotion could not represent unsuccessful Hispanic applicants for the position. In *Kremer v Chemical Construction Corp.*,[37] the Court extended principles of comity to rule that rejection of a Title VII claim by a state agency may preclude assertion of a federal action on the claim, even though state courts would not review the merits of the agency decision.[38]

35. 104 S. Ct. at 2235. The Court cited Norwood v. Harrison, 413 U.S. 455 (1973)(state cannot give financial support to private, segregated schools); Runyon v. McCrary, 427 U.S. 160 (1976) (civil rights statute bars private, segregated school from refusing to admit black children); Railway Mail Assn. v. Corsi, 326 U.S. 88 (1945)(labor union may not discriminate against black employees).

Justice Powell concurred briefly in *Hishon* to make clear his view that the case not be read as extending Title VII to the management of a law firm by its partners. 104 S. Ct. at 2236. He also noted that while, as the Court asserted, "invidious private discrimination was not afforded affirmative consitutional protection," this did not mean that the enforcement of such laws "will always be without cost to other values, including constitutional rights." "Such laws," Justice Powell said, " may impede the exercise of personal judgment in choosing one's associates or colleagues." *Id.* at 2236, n.4.

36. 457 U.S. 147 (1982).

37. 456 U.S. 461 (1982).

38. Justices Blackmun, Brennan, Marshall, and Stevens dissented, asserting that Title VII itself anticipates actions after unsuccessful state agency or court proceedings. They warned that the decision will make state proceedings a "complainant's sole remedy when he unsuccessfully pursues judicial review" in the state courts. *Id.* at 480. *See also* Note, *A Tragi-Comity: Kremer v. Chemical Construction Corp.*, 15 Conn. L. Rev. 799 (1983) (the Supreme Court chose to affirm the Second Circuit rather than adopt the rule of four other circuits that had ruled against such preclusion).

Texas Dept. of Community Affairs v. Burdine[39] and *U.S. Postal Service Board of Governors v. Aikens*[40] considered the requirements and effect of the plaintiff's prima facie case. *Burdine* held that establishing a prima facie case does not shift the burden of persuasion to the defendant but merely requires the defendant to present clearly nondiscriminatory reasons for its actions. The *Aikens* opinion castigated the lower courts for focusing on the prima facie case without reaching the essential question of racial discrimination. Another case restricted remedies available under Title VII.

In *Ford Motor Co. v. EEOC*,[41] the Court ruled that an employer can toll accrual of backpay on a discrimination claim by offering a comparable position without retroactive seniority. The Court was concerned that requiring retroactive seniority would discourage employers from settling claims, and that it would injure the rights of current employees. Commentators criticized the Court for valuing the seniority rights of victims of discrimination lower than those of employees who would not have gained seniority absent the discriminatory acts.[42]

The general tenor of these decisions is to restrict entry into court, to increase the plaintiff's burden, and to restrict remedies available to successful plaintiffs. The Court's approach is in striking contrast to the liberal construction given Title VII in its early years.[43] Yet in certain cases the Supreme Court seems willing to rule liberally. In *Connecticut v. Teal*,[44] for example, the Court refused to accept an employer's "bottom line" argument that nondiscriminatory policies regarding entry level positions were a defense to charges of discriminatory promotion policies. The decision held that the use of a written examination that excluded a disproportionate number of minorities from consideration for promotion violated Title VII.[45] The case is a welcome precedent for those concerned that affirmative action programs have little influence beyond the entry level.

There is no single explanation for the mixed signals sent by these decisions. The Court's ideological split on civil rights issues continues un-

39. 450 U.S. 248 (1981).

40. 460 U.S. 711 (1983).

41. 458 U.S. 219 (1982).

42. *See* Note, *Diluting Relief Under Title VII: Ford Motor Co. v. Equal Employment Opportunity Commission — Employment Offer Absent Retroactive Seniority Effective in Tolling Backpay*, 32 Cath. U. L. Rev. 665 (1983); Comment, *Ford's Got a Better Idea?: How to Toll Back Pay Liability to Title VII Claimants: Ford Motor Co. v. EEOC*, 4 U. Bridgeport L. Rev. 311 (1983); Note, *Ford Motor Company v. EEOC: A Setback for Victims of Discrimination*, 44 U. Pitt. L. Rev. 707 (1983).

43. Comment, *Title VII Class Actions: A New Era?*, 62 Neb. L. Rev. 130, 131 (1983).

44. 457 U.S. 440 (1982). *Teal* was followed by the Ninth Circuit in Peters v. Lieuallen, 693 F.2d 966 (9th Cir. 1982).

45. The Court affirmed the Second Circuit's approach on this point, though most circuits had refused to consider an examination's effect separately from the total selection process.

abated, and the presence of swing votes ensures inconsistent results.[46] Many of the Court's restrictive decisions seem prompted by a desire to control the deluge of civil rights cases in recent years, alleging every conceivable type of discrimination.[47] Most commentators, however, are critical of the use of restrictive procedural requirements that act to bar both frivolous and meritorious claims.[48] At heart, many of the cases seem to reflect an unwillingness that has been evident since *Washington v. Davis*[49] to further expand remedies for discrimination. Discrimination claims, when they are dramatic enough, and do not greatly threaten majority concerns, are given a sympathetic hearing, but there is a pervasive sense that definite limits have been set on the weight that minority claims receive when balanced against majority interests.

§9.11.3 Voluntary Affirmative Action: Update

Though in widespread use, affirmative action plans are the subject of much debate. The state of the law in this area is unsettled, to say the least. It is clear that after *Weber*[50] private employer affirmative action plans may not be challenged unless they unduly burden majority employees.[51] Where state action is involved, affirmative action programs must meet Fourteenth Amendment equal protection standards as well as Title VII, but the courts have been unable to agree on the proper equal protection analysis for affirmative action plans adopted by governmental bodies. The Supreme

46. Justice O'Connor, for instance, though generally of conservative views, is particularly interested in women's issues and has used her vote to control the result in cases such as *Arizona Governing Committee for Tax Deferred Annuity and Deferred Compensation Plans v. Norris*, 103 S. Ct. 3492 (1983)(struck down sex-based differences in annuity payments by a 5-4 majority, but O'Connor voted with the dissent to prevent retroactive application of the decision).

47. *See* discussion of 42 U.S.C. §1983 in Chapter 5.

48. *See* Note, *A Tragi-Comity: Kremer v. Chemical Construction Corp.*, 15 Conn. L. Rev. 799 (1983). Comment, *Title VII Class Actions: A New Era?*, 62 Neb. L. Rev. 130 1983). Note, *Ford Motor Company v. EEOC: A Setback for Victims of Discrimination*, 44 U. Pitt. L. Rev. 707 (1983). *Cf.* Note, *The Bottom Line Concept in Title VII Litigation: Connecticut v. Teal and the Relevance of End Results*, 15 Conn. L. Rev. 821 (1983).

One alternative to strict procedural requirements that may stem the flow of discrimination claims is the incipient development of employment law theories that accommodate workers whose claim is not rooted in class-based discrimination. *See* Note, *Wrongful Termination of Employees at Will—The California Trend*, 78 Nw. U. L. Rev. 259 (1983).

49. 426 U.S. 229 (1976).

50. United Steelworkers of America v. Weber, 443 U.S. 193 (1979).

51. Voluntarily adopted private employer affirmative action plans may include elements of racial preference such as numerical goals or quotas if they do not unduly trammel majority employees' rights. 443 U.S. at 208.

Court, though approving of the general principle of voluntary affirmative action, has avoided several opportunities to set clear rules for the circuits.[52] At least one writer suggests that the Supreme Court has intentionally analyzed affirmative action plans in a vague and muddled fashion so as to preserve the freedom to reconsider its support for affirmative action when it no longer seems necessary.[53]

The controversy regarding public affirmative action plans centers around several interrelated issues: the legitimate goals of an affirmative action plan; the authority necessary to implement a program involving racial preference; and the findings necessary to support a plan based on remediation of past discrimination. Though *Bakke* is a weak precedent at best,[54] we can reason by analogy that a governmental employer can use race as a factor in hiring decisions if supported by a strong state interest. Several federal decisions have found approximation of the community's racial composition in a governmental work force to be such an interest, particularly for law enforcement and public contact jobs.[55] The remediation of disparities in the employment of protected groups caused by past discrimination is also a legitimate interest, and perhaps the most generally recognized goal of affirmative action.[56]

It is a more difficult question to determine what bodies have the authority to initiate affirmative action extending past that approved in *Bakke*. That case spoke of a determination by a judicial, legislative, or administrative body.[57] The Supreme Court's decision in *Fullilove v. Klutznick*[58] indicates that congressionally authorized affirmative action programs are to receive the most deferential treatment. Affirmative action programs created by state and local legislatures are similarly treated by the courts, as are programs implemented under court order.[59] The authority of administrative agencies is the least certain. Some jurisdictions have indicated that ad-

52. Bohrer, *Bakke, Weber, and Fullilove: Benign Discrimination and Congressional Power to Enforce the Fourteenth Amendment*, 56 Ind. L.J. 473, 511 (1981).

53. Comment, *Reverse Racial Preferences Under the Equal Protection Clause: Round II, Fullilove v. Klutznick*, 19 Am. Bus. L.J. 197, 212 (1981).

54. Regents of the University of California v. Bakke, 438 U.S. 265 (1978). *Bakke* is a weak precedent not only because it concerned education rather than employment, but because it was a plurality decision with no one opinion speaking for a majority of the court.

55. *See, e.g.*, Talbert v. City of Richmond, 648 F.2d 925, 931 (4th Cir. 1981); Castro v. Beecher, 365 F. Supp. 655, 659 (D. Mass. 1973).

56. Other goals that have received less support are simple proportional representation of racial groups in public employment and service to the minority community. Reynolds v. Sheet Metal Workers Local 102, 498 F. Supp. 952 (D.D.C. 1980), *aff'd*, 702 F.2d 221 (D.C. Cir. 1981). *See also* Dixon, *Bakke: A Constitutional Analysis*, 67 Cal. L. Rev. 69, 77 (1979).

57. 438 U.S. at 307.

58. 448 U.S. 448 (1980).

59. Bratton v. City of Detroit, 704 F.2d 878 (6th Cir. 1983), *cert. denied*, 104 S. Ct. 703 (1984); Valentine v. Smith, 654 F.2d 503 (8th Cir. 1981).

ministrative agencies have only limited authority to adopt affirmative action plans without legislative or judicial approval, but such programs have also been upheld.[60]

In most federal cases "voluntary" affirmative action plans have been adopted after a judicial determination of past discrimination.[61] Often the governmental entity involved has participated in overt discrimination. In these cases little discussion is needed of the adequacy of the factual basis for remedial action. The federal appeals courts have not addressed another case like *Bakke*, where an administrative agency embarked on an affirmative action program entailing racial preference without determination of its own past discrimination. The acceptability of programs adopted without findings of past discrimination or some other justification is thus subject to doubt, and lower federal courts have not ruled uniformly.[62] However, the support voiced by many federal courts for voluntary adoption of affirmative action plans cuts against any requirement of official admission or determination of past discrimination, since such a requirement would discourage compliance by opening up public employers to further liability.[63] Federal courts also vary in their willingness to accept societal discrimination or mere numerical underrepresentation of minorities as justification for remedial affirmative action programs.[64] However, when programs were initiated by a legislative body, whether federal, state, or local, courts have accepted the findings of discrimination, however vague, as adequate.[65]

In the absence of federal guidance, many state and local governments have nonetheless instituted affirmative action plans. When challenged, these have received disparate treatment in the courts, but a

60. *See* La Riviere v. EEOC, 682 F.2d 1275 (9th Cir. 1982); Marrotta v. Usery, 629 F.2d (9th Cir. 1980).

61. *See, e.g.*, Bratton v. City of Detroit, 704 F.2d 878 (6th Cir. 1983), *cert. denied*, 104 S. Ct. 703 (1984).

62. *See* Valentine v. Smith, 654 F.2d 503 (8th Cir. 1981), *cert. denied*, 454 U S. 1124 (1981) (court ordered faculty desegregation at Arkansas State University); United States v. City of Miami, 614 F.2d 1322 (5th Cir. 1980), *modified*, 664 F.2d 435 (1981)(consent decree).

63. The Supreme Court has referred to the "extremely high premium put by Congress on voluntary settlement of Title VII suits." Albemarle Paper Co. v. Moody, 422 U.S. 405, 418 (1975). *See also* United States v. City of Miami, 614 F.2d 1322, 1331 (5th Cir. 1980), *modified*, 664 F.2d 435 (1981).

64. *See* Van Aken v. Young, 541 F. Supp. 448 (E.D. Mich. 1982) (upholding plan based on societal discrimination); Reichman v. Bureau of Affirmative Action, 536 F. Supp. 1149 (M.D. Pa. 1982). *Compare* Valentine v. Drug Enforcement Admin., 544 F. Supp. 830 (D. Ill. 1982); Central Paving, Inc. v. James, 499 F. Supp. 629 (M.D. Ala. 1980). Some state cases seem to indicate a greater willingness to accept vague findings of inadvertent or societal discrimination as sufficient. *See* discussion, *infra* this section.

65. Fullilove v. Klutznick, 448 U.S. 448 (1980); M. C. West, Inc. v. Lewis, 522 F. Supp. 338 (M.D. Tenn. 1981).

surprising number of truly voluntary programs have been upheld.[66] In *Maehren v. City of Seattle*,[67] the Washington Supreme Court upheld an affirmative action plan covering employees of the City of Seattle against equal protection and Title VII challenges. The plan, which used "selective certification" of qualified minority applicants from a separately maintained list, was adopted voluntarily by a Seattle agency in response to Executive Order 11246[68] and Washington State enactments prohibiting discrimination.[69] The court held that statistical underrepresentation of minorities in city employment was a valid basis for the inference that past selection processes had discriminated against minority applicants.[70]

The California Supreme Court approved a similar preferential hiring plan in *Price v. Civil Service Commn. of Sacramento County*.[71] The plan was adopted by the Sacramento County Civil Service Commission on its own determination that "inadvertently discriminatory" features of its hiring process in the past had resulted in disproportionately low minority employment.[72] The plan was individually tailored to the needs of various departments in the County; the particular practice upheld was a ratio calculated to ensure that one third of the new hirees in the district attorney's office would be minorities.[73]

In *Portland Police Association v. Civil Service Board*,[74] the Oregon Supreme Court upheld an affirmative action plan which used a double list system for hiring and promotion. The Portland Civil Service Board had adopted the plan on its own finding that discriminatory procedures in the past had limited minority access to city employment. The court held that although the issue of the agency's authority to institute such a plan was not thoroughly established, the plan itself was not precluded by state or federal law, including the Fourteenth Amendment.

66. *Cf.* Chmill v. City of Pittsburgh, 488 Pa. 470, 412 A.2d 860 (1980)(upheld program only because there had been prior judicial determination of liability).

67. 92 Wash. 2d 480, 599 P.2d 1255 (1979), *cert. denied*, 452 U.S. 938 (1981).

68. Exec. Order 11,246, 3 C.F.R. 611 (1965), *reprinted in*, 42 U.S.C. §2000e (1982).

69. Wash. Rev. Code Ann. Ch. 49.60 (1983).

70. 92 Wash. 2d at 495, 599 P.2d at 1265.

71. 26 Cal. 3d 257, 161 Cal. Rptr. 475, 604 P.2d 1365, *cert. dismissed*, 449 U.S. 811 (1980).

72. *Id.* at 263, 161 Cal. Rptr. at 478, 604 P.2d at 1368.

73. *Id.* at 265, 161 Cal. Rptr. at 480, 604 P.2d at 1370.

74. 292 Or. 433, 639 P.2d 619 (1982). The court declined to rule whether the agency had authority to implement the plan on its own initiative, and whether its findings of discrimination had been sufficient. *Id.* at 449, 639 P.2d at 628.

§9.11.3a Affirmative Action vs. Seniority Rights

Some of the thorniest problems in employment law arise from the tension between affirmative action goals and seniority rights. These problems take various forms: conflicts between affirmative action plans and seniority-based promotions;[75] rights of victims of discrimination to retroactive seniority;[76] and erasure of minority employment gains by "last-hired, first fired" layoff requirements.[77] Most affirmative action programs do not disturb seniority rights guaranteed by labor agreements or local statutes.[78] Yet, to be successful affirmative action must interfere to some degree with seniority rights.[79]

The federal courts are now grappling with a series of cases that polarize the issues involved. In the last few years a number of cities have been forced by financial crisis to lay off public employees.[80] These cities have been faced with the choice of whether to violate union contracts and local statutes requiring seniority-based layoffs or to erase recent gains in minority employment produced by court approved affirmative action plans. The experience of Boston is typical.[81] During the 1970's Boston was found liable for past employment discrimination,[82] and subsequently a consent order

75. *See* Bratton v. City of Detroit, 704 F.2d 878 (6th Cir. 1983), *cert. denied*, 104 S. Ct. 703 (1984).

76. *See* Ford Motor Co. v. EEOC, 458 U.S. 219 (1982).

77. The cases discussed in this section involve principally public employees. For a case discussing layoffs by private employers, *see* W. R. Grace & Co. v. Local Union 759, 461 U.S. 757 (1983) (discussed in §9.3.1).

78. Brown v. Neeb, 644 F.2d 551, 560 (6th Cir. 1981).

79. This is especially true in times of economic scarcity, when layoffs are a fact of life and there are not enough good jobs to go around. Even in cases where minority workers are given equal seniority rather than preference over white workers, there is increased competition for promotions and less safety from layoffs. *The Wall Street Journal*, Mar. 23, 1983, p.33.

Courts treat the balance of equities as shifting in different situations. Minority workers who can prove that discrimination prevented their hiring or promotion have a clear claim to seniority over employees hired or promoted since the discriminatory act. The same would seem to be true where a general policy of exclusion (by the employer or by society) has prevented minorities from establishing seniority, yet in these cases courts tend to weigh the expectations of "innocent" whites who benefited from the discrimination more heavily. *See* Note, *Ford Motor Company v. EEOC: A Setback for Victims of Discrimination*, 44 U. Pitt. L. Rev. 707 (1983).

80. A partial list of the cities affected includes Boston, Cincinnati, Detroit, Memphis, Miami, and Toledo.

81. The following facts are taken from NAACP v. Beecher, 679 F.2d 965 (1st Cir. 1982), *vac. as moot, sub nom.* Boston Firefighters Union v. NAACP, 461 U.S. 477 (1983).

82. There are numerous reported decisions in the Boston employee cases. The two main lines of decision are: Castro v. Beecher, 334 F. Supp. 930 (D. Mass. 1971), *aff'd*, 459 F.2d 725 (1st Cir. 1972); NAACP v. Beecher, 371 F. Supp. 507 (D. Mass.), *aff'd*, 504 F.2d 1017 (1st Cir. 1974), *cert. denied*, 421 U.S. 910 (1975).

was entered mandating increased black and Hispanic employment.[83] In July 1981 the city announced seniority-based layoffs that would affect about 48 percent of its black and Hispanic city employees. The Boston NAACP filed suit to prevent the layoffs, arguing that they would destroy recent gains made through affirmative action. The district court found that the proposed layoffs were a new and unforeseen circumstance, and modified the consent decree to forbid reduction of black and Hispanic employment below the existing percentages.[84]

The First Circuit affirmed this decision in an eloquent and humane opinion by Justice Bownes,[85] citing the lower court's inherent equity power to modify its consent decree to reflect unforeseen circumstances.[86] The court found that a Massachusetts statute requiring seniority-based layoffs was preempted by the need to prevent evisceration of the remedy provided by the consent decree,[87] and that nothing in prior Supreme Court cases precluded this result.[88] Justice Bownes wrote: "The layoffs here were bound to cause undeserved injury in any event. . . . [T]here is nothing magical about seniority, and here common sense suggests that it should be tempered by other entirely rational considerations so that the racial equality achieved at considerable effort in the past decade not be erased."[89]

The other circuits that have addressed these issues have ruled similarly.[90] The Supreme Court granted certiorari in the Boston case, but later vacated the decision as moot after Massachusetts appropriated money to hire back all laid-off employees.[91] Then in the Memphis case, *Firefighters Local Union No. 1784 v. Stotts*,[92] the Court reached a contrary conclusion in a case involving almost identical facts. The Sixth Circuit had held in *Stotts* that consent decrees may be modified on a showing of changed circumstances or inequity,[93] and that the issuing court has a duty to ensure

83. Castro v. Beecher, 365 F. Supp. 655 (D. Mass. 1973); NAACP v. Beecher, 371 F. Supp. 507 (D. Mass. 1974). Both decrees were amended and supplemented during the late 1970's. 679 F.2d at 968.

84. Castro v. Beecher, 522 F. Supp. 873, 877 (D. Mass. 1981).

85. NAACP v. Beecher, 679 F.2d 965 (1st Cir. 1982).

86. *Id.* at 972.

87. *Id.* at 974.

88. *Id.*

89. *Id.* at 978.

90. Guardians Assoc. v. Civil Service Commn. 633 F.2d 232 (2d Cir. 1980)(affirmed Title VII portion of case); Memphis Fire Dept. v. Stotts, 679 F.2d 541 (6th Cir. 1982); Brown v. Neeb, 644 F.2d 551 (6th Cir. 1981). Two cases seem to reach a contrary result because liability of the city was never determined, but use a consistent rationale: Youngblood v. Dalzell, 568 F.2d 506 (6th Cir. 1978)(consent decree expressly disclaimed liability); United States v. City of Miami, 614 F.2d 1322 (5th Cir. 1980), *modified*, 664 F.2d 435 (1981).

91. Boston Firefighters Union v. NAACP, 461 U.S. 477 (1983).

92. 104 S. Ct. 2576 (1984).

93. 679 F. 2d 541, 561 (6th Cir. 1982).

that the terms of its consent decrees are carried out.[94] Courts may approve modifications that conflict with collective bargaining provisions, even with a bona fide seniority system, to prevent frustration of an affirmative action plan.[95] Nonminority employees benefited from, and acquiesced in, past discrimination by the city, and therefore have no basis to protest reasonable steps taken to remedy the adverse affects of discrimination on minorities.[96]

The thrust of Justice White's opinion was that the district court lacked authority under either Title VII or the consent degree to modify that order so as to displace white employees with seniority in favor of blacks with less seniority. He rejected the Eighth Circuit's specific performance approach by pointing out that the consent degree made no mention of layoffs or demotions, or that the parties understood that the city would be able to simply ignore its last hired, first fired seniority arrangement with the union if layoffs took place.

For similar reasons, Justice White also rejected the argument that the injunction properly carried out the purposes of the degree which nowhere mentioned the displacement of white employees with seniority over blacks. Title VII, he pointed out, protects bona fide seniority systems, and it is inappropriate in a pattern or practice suit "to deny an innocent employee the benefits of his seniority in order to provide a remedy." Finally, he noted that any implied settlement approach ignores the fact that neither the union nor the city were parties to the original settlement between black employees and the fire department.[97]

Justice Blackmun, joined by Justices Brennan and Marshall, dissented. He argued the case was moot and any continuing effects on the city would be ended if the Court followed its usual procedure of vacating the court of appeals' judgment. The district court had not heard the case on the merits, and the Supreme Court should not have done so. Even assuming the Court had jurisdiction to review, Justice Blackmun said, the only question was whether the district court abused its discretion in applying the usual standards for granting preliminary relief: the plaintiffs' likelihood of success on the merits, the balance of irreparable harm to the parties, and whether the injunction would be in the public interest.

On the merits, Blackmun denied that the injunction required the city to layoff any white employees at all. Several parties, including the union, urged the city to avoid layoffs by reducing the working hours of all fire department employees. The injunction did not abrogate the contractual

94. *Id.* at 557.
95. *Id.* at 564.
96. *Id.* at 559.
97. Justices O'Connor and Stevens concurred on both the merits and the hotly contested issue over whether the case should have been dismissed as moot because the recession is over, employees layed off or demoted under the injunction have been returned to their jobs, and the City has no current need to make seniority-based layoffs.

rights of white employees, and if the city's layoff plan infringed on those rights, the union retained the power to enforce them, citing *W.R. Grace & Co. v. Local Union 759.*[98]

Had the district court entered a permanent injunction, Justice Blackmun felt either of the two approaches adopted by the Eighth Circuit justified the district court's action. Moreover, he argued, the majority ignored the 1972 amendments to §706(g) that earlier had been read to bar race-conscious relief. He said the provision was broadened to authorize courts to order "such affirmative action as may be appropriate, which may include, *but is not limited to,* reinstatement or hiring of employees, with or without back-pay . . . *or any other equitable relief as the court deems appropriate.*" (emphasis added by the opinion).[99] He added that the Senate had rejected an amendment that would have prohibited governmental agencies from requiring employers to adopt goals or quotas for the hiring of minorities.

Two 1982 decisions interpreted Title VII's exception for bona fide seniority plans generously.[100] In *American Tobacco Co. v. Patterson*[101] a 5-4 majority refused to examine seniority systems created after the 1964 effective date of Title VII more closely than pre-existing seniority systems, even when the employer engaged in overt discrimination prior to enactment. In 1968 the defendant American Tobacco Co. adopted a seniority-based promotion system along nine lines of progression that effectively insulated white-held "top jobs" from entry by blacks.[102] The union, which had maintained segregated locals prior to the enactment of Title VII, assented in the adoption of this system.[103] The case was remanded to determine whether the seniority system was intentionally discriminatory. Justice Stevens dissented, reasoning that "a seniority system that is unlawful at the time it is adopted cannot be bona fide within the meaning of §703(h)," so that a post-Act system that produces a discriminatory effect could not fall within Title VII's exemption.[104]

In *Pullman-Standard v. Swint*[105] black employees of a railroad car manufacturer challenged a seniority system that perpetuated the effects of pre-Title VII discrimination.[106] Seniority was measured by length of ser-

98. 461 U.S. 757 (1983). *See* discussion *supra* §9.3.1.

99. 104 S. Ct. at 2609.

100. Civil Rights Act of 1964, §703(h), 42 U.S.C. §2000e-2(h) (1976 & Supp IV 1981), exempts unintentional discrimination if the discriminatory practice is part of a bona fide seniority system. Section 703(h) reverses the general policy of Title VII which otherwise does not distinguish between intentional and unintentional discrimination.

101. 456 U.S. 63 (1982).

102. *Id.* at 66.

103. *Id.*

104. *Id.* at 87-88.

105. 456 U.S. 273 (1982)

106. *Id.* at 278.

vice in a particular department; employees transferring to new departments lost seniority, so blacks were hesitant to apply for desegregated positions.[107] The Court held that the Fifth Circuit had overstepped its authority by reversing the trial court's finding that the seniority system was not discriminatory, and that intent to discriminate was a pure question of fact rather than a mixed fact-law question as the Fifth Circuit had ruled.[108]

These decisions indicate certain tendencies of the Supreme Court in weighing seniority rights against minority rights, but are by no means dispositive. The impressive consistency of the circuits in justifying modification of seniority rights to preserve affirmative action argues for affirmance of *Stotts*. In addition, the cases just discussed did not present such a direct threat to affirmative action plans as the seniority layoff cases. The Supreme Court has shown a general (if rather murky) intent to support affirmative action as a remedial measure.[109] Though both rights involved are valid, surely the equities favor enforcement of remedies for past discrimination. As Justice Bownes wrote in the Boston case: "To a minority police officer or fire fighter hired within the last ten years, the imposition of a rigid last hired, first fired seniority system would only mean that once again the dominant white culture had protected its own kind at the expense of blacks and hispanics."[110]

§9.11.4 Minority Business Enterprises: Recent Cases

In *Fullilove v. Klutznick*,[111] a plurality of the Supreme Court upheld the Minority Business Enterprise provision discussed in the Second Edition §9.11.4, Chief Justice Burger announced the judgment of the Court and delivered an opinion joined by Justices White and Powell. The Chief Justice did not use the common terminology of equal protection analysis, but stressed the deference due to congressional exercises of power.[112] Though Congress had not made explicit findings of past discrimination, the Court found that the program was remedial in nature.[113] Justice Powell also concurred separately, to emphasize the need for articulated standards of review.[114] Justice Marshall's concurring opinion, supporting an intermediate standard of scrutiny in affirmative action cases, was joined by Justices Bren-

107. *Id.* at 278-279.
108. *Id.* at 287, 288.
109. *See* Fullilove v. Klutznick, 448 U.S. 448 (1980); United Steelworkers of America v. Weber, 443 U.S. 193 (1979); Regents of the Univ. of Calif. v. Bakke, 438 U.S. 265 (1978).
110. 679 F.2d at 978.
111. 448 U.S. 448 (1980), *aff'g* Fullilove v. Kreps, 584 F.2d 600 (2d Cir. 1978).
112. *Id.* at 472.
113. *Id.* at 463, 467.
114. *Id.* at 495.

nan and Blackmun.[115] Justice Stewart, joined by Justice Rehnquist dissented, and Justice Stevens dissented separately. The case, thus, is an example of both the Court's ideological split and the proliferation of multiple concurrences and dissents.

Law review commentary on *Fullilove* was mixed. Though the case received much comment, the plurality opinion ensured that no consensus would be possible as to what it actually meant. Most authors criticized the Court for failing to establish a clear standard for scrutiny of affirmative action programs, though few criticized the outcome of the case.[116] One writer hailed the Court's incomprehensible affirmative action policy as a deliberate and practical choice which allowed it to uphold affirmative action plans for the present while preserving the freedom to reconsider such policies in the future.[117] The Court's deference to Congress was both praised and attacked.[118]

Cases after *Fullilove* have mirrored the commentators' confusion as to its holding. *Fullilove*'s validation of the federal MBE program inspired similar programs initiated at every level of government: state, local, and federal and state agencies. Most courts have held that any legislative body, state or federal, has the power to initiate a reasonable MBE program.[119] Some of these courts reflect a very deferential approach to legislative findings of fact and determinations of reasonable means, even when the legislative body is only a local government.[120] Other courts would take a harder look at the qualifications of the initiating body, its factual basis for action, and the terms of the program.[121]

The power of agencies to initiate MBE programs without legislative authorization is more doubtful. *Central Alabama Paving, Inc. v. James*,[122] enjoined enforcement of regulations issued by the federal Department of

115. 448 U.S. at 517.

116. *See* Comment, *Fullilove and the Minority Set Aside: In Search of an Affirmative Action Rationale*, 29 Emory L.J. 1127 (1980); Bohrer, *Bakke, Weber and Fullilove: Benign Discrimination and Congressional Power to Enforce the Fourteenth Amendment*, 56 Ind. L.J. 473 (1981); Note, *Constitutional Law — Strictly Scrutinizing Fullilove v. Klutznick*, 60 N.C. L. Rev. 681 (1982).

117. Comment, *Reverse Racial Preferences Under the Equal Protection Clause: Round II, Fullilove v. Klutznick*, 19 Am. Bus. L.J. 197 (1981).

118. *See* Note *The Constitutionality of Affirmative Action in Public Employment: Judicial Deference to Certain Politically Responsible Bodies*, 67 Va. L. Rev. 1235 (1981); Note, *Fullilove v. Klutznick: Do Affirmative Action Plans Require Congressional Authorization?*, 38 Wash. & Lee L. Rev. 1315 (1981).

119. *See* Ohio Contractors Assoc. v. Keip, 713 F.2d 167 (6th Cir. 1983); Southwest Washington Chapter, National Electrical Contractors Assn. v. Pierce County, 100 Wash. 2d 109, 667 P.2d 1092 (1983).

120. *See, e.g.*, Michigan Road Builders Assn. v. Milliken, 571 F. Supp. 173 (E.D. Mich. 1983).

121. *See, e.g.*, South Florida Chapter of the Assoc. General Contractors of America, Inc. v. Metropolitan Dade County, 723 F.2d 846 (11th Cir. 1984).

122. 499 F. Supp. 629 (M.D. Ala. 1980).

Transportation (DOT) that required state highway departments to follow MBE goals established by the DOT. The court distinguished the case from *Fullilove* by holding that such programs violated equal protection unless adopted by agencies under congressional authorization or after a finding of past discrimination by a federal agency.[123] The opinion indicated an assumption that only federally initiated MBE programs would be constitutional.[124]

The impact of *James* was softened somewhat by a subsequent case, *M.C. West, Inc. v. Lewis*,[125] which upheld the validity of the same DOT regulations after approval by the U. S. Attorney General and certain amendments.[126] The court could find no certain source of statutory authority for the DOT regulations, but held that the DOT had made sufficient findings of discrimination in hearings before amending the regulations.[127] The Ninth Circuit has eschewed the strict approach of *James* altogether, and in *Schmidt v. Oakland Unified School District*, upheld a MBE program adopted on the initiative of a local school board rather than by a state or federal legislature.

123. *Id.* at 636. The injunction in *James* was granted partly because the U.S. Attorney General had not yet approved the DOT regulations as required by Title VI. The Attorney General did subsequently approve the regulations. M. C. West. Inc. v. Lewis, 522 F. Supp. 338, 345 n.8 (M.D. Tenn. 1981).

124. 499 F. Supp. at 637.

125. 522 F.Supp. 338 (M.D. Tenn. 1981).

126. *Id.* at 349.

127. 662 F.2d 550 (9th Cir. 1981), *vac. on other grounds*, 457 U.S. 594 (1982).